NEW PATHS TO POWER

AMERICAN WOMEN
1890-1920

GIVE HER OF THE FRUIT
OF HER HANDS, AND LET ·
HER OWN WORKS PRAISE,
· HER IN THE GATES.

THE YOUNG OXFORD HISTORY OF WOMEN IN THE UNITED STATES

Nancy F. Cott, *General Editor*

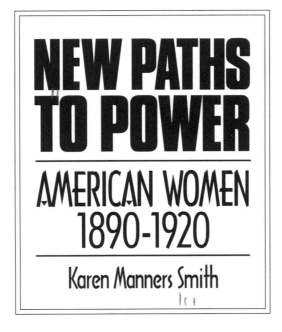

NEW PATHS TO POWER

AMERICAN WOMEN
1890-1920

Karen Manners Smith

OXFORD UNIVERSITY PRESS

New York • Oxford

To my father, Robert A. Manners,
with love and thanks

Oxford University Press

Oxford   New York   Toronto
Delhi   Bombay   Calcutta   Madras   Karachi
Kuala Lumpur   Singapore   Hong Kong   Tokyo
Nairobi   Dar es Salaam   Cape Town
Melbourne   Auckland   Madrid
and associated companies in
Berlin   Ibadan

Published by Oxford University Press, Inc.,
200 Madison Avenue, New York, New York 10016

Oxford is a registered trademark of Oxford University Press, Inc.

Library of Congress Cataloging-in-Publication Data

Smith, Karen Manners.
New Paths to Power : American women 1890-1920 / Karen Manners Smith.
p. cm. — (The Young Oxford history of women in the United States ; v. 7)
Includes bibliographical references and index.
ISBN 0-19-508111-0
ISBN 0-19-508830-1 (series)
1. Women—United States—History—20th century—Juvenile literature. 2. Women—United States—Social conditions—
Juvenile literature. 3. Feminism—United States—History—Juvenile literature. 4. United States—Social conditions—
1865-1918—Juvenile literature. [1. Women—History—20th century. 2. Women—Social conditions.
3. United States—Social conditions—1865-1918.]
I. Title. II Series.
HQ1419.S57   1994
305.4'0973'09041—dc20   93-33598
                                                                                                              CIP
                                                                                                              AC

1 3 5 7 9 8 6 4 2
Printed in the United States of America
on acid-free paper

Design: Leonard Levitsky
Picture research: Lisa Kirchner, Laura Kreiss

On the cover: A publication of the National American Woman Suffrage Association, 1915.
Frontispiece: The back cover of *The Woman Citizen*, October 20, 1917, published by the National American
Woman Suffrage Association.

CONTENTS

INTRODUCTION

I n the United States, the turn from the 19th to the 20th century marked a time of industrial consolidation, tremendous immigration from Europe, and migration from farms to cities. The consequences could be seen in new extremes of wealth and poverty, much greater religious and cultural variety, and broader differences in education, sophistication, and occupational distinctions among the population. Almost two-thirds of the nation worked not on farms but instead in heavy industries, in manufacturing and trade, in shops, offices, banks, schools, government agencies, and large corporations.

Technological innovation vastly changed people's styles of living: photography, electricity, gas lighting, the telegraph and the telephone came into use by the close of the 19th century; the 20th century quickly added the automobile, airplane, electric railway, wireless radio, and moving pictures. Through growth in population and resources, through war and economic force, the United States asserted itself as a power in the world.

As this book tells in lively detail, these were years for women's educational, occupational, and professional advancement. Girls and women (many of them immigrants or the daughters of immigrants) swelled the growing ranks of wage earners and of high school and

Women operatives press flowers in a New York factory. The working conditions were often primitive, the hours were long, and the women were paid by the piece.

college students. Women increased their proportions in the professions: one could find not only women novelists and grammar-school teachers but also women doctors and lawyers, public health officers and social investigators, architects, newspaperwomen, and college professors. Just as striking was women's voluntary activity at the local level, in clubs, associations, cooperatives, leagues, and groups organized for purposes from self-help to charity to group advancement to overall social reform. Perhaps the characteristic voluntary association of the age was the settlement house, where women college graduates established homes in immigrant quarters of major cities, becoming resident social researchers and sympathetic neighbors at the same time. These local associations also joined in state and national federations. The National American Woman Suffrage Association, the National Association of Colored Women, the General Federation of Women's Clubs, the National Consumer's League, and the National Women's Trade Union League all date from this era.

This book is part of a series that covers the history of women in

Suffrage campaigners in St. Louis prepare for a march. In the summer of 1919 Missouri became one of the first states to ratify the 19th Amendment.

the United States from the 17th through 20th century. Traditional historical writing has dealt almost entirely with men's lives because men have, until very recently, been the heads of state, the political officials, judges, ministers, and business leaders who have wielded the most visible and recorded power. But for several recent decades, new interest has arisen in social and cultural history, where common people are the actors who create trends and mark change as well as continuity. An outpouring of research and writing on women's history has been part of this trend to look at individuals and groups who have not held the reins of rule in their own hands but nonetheless participated in making history. The motive to address and correct sexual inequality in society has also vitally influenced women's history, on the thinking that knowledge of the past is essential to creating justice for the future.

The histories in this series look at many aspects of women's lives. The books ask new questions about the course of American history. How did the type and size of families change, and what difference did that make in people's lives? What expectations for women differed from those for men, and how did such expectations change over the centuries? What roles did women play in the economy? What form did women's political participation take when they could not vote? And how did politics change when women did gain full citizenship? How did women work with other women who were like or unlike them, as well as with men, for social and political goals? What sex-specific constraints or opportunities did they face? The series aims to understand the diverse women who have peopled American history by investigating their work and leisure, family patterns, political activities, forms of organization, and outstanding accomplishments. Standard events of American history, from the settling of the continent to the American revolution, the Civil War, industrialization, American entry onto the world stage, and world wars, are all here, too, but seen from the point of view of women's experiences. Together, the answers to new questions and the treatment of old ones from women's points of view make up a compelling narrative of four centuries of history in the United States.

—Nancy F. Cott

THE YOUNG OXFORD HISTORY OF WOMEN IN THE UNITED STATES

CHAPTER 1

PROLOGUE:
WOMEN AND THE WORLD'S COLUMBIAN EXPOSITION OF 1893

In the summer of 1893, more than 27 million women, men, and children from all over the world visited the World's Columbian Exposition in Chicago. The fairgrounds, containing exhibits from 72 countries, covered 633 acres of Jackson Park, a few miles south of the city center. Grouped around a series of artificial lagoons, where waterfowl swam alongside imported Venetian gondolas, were the glittering palaces of the "White City," 12 vast, Classical-style pavilions dedicated to America's industries, its agricultural and mining developments, its fine arts, and the new miracle of electricity. The Manufactures and Liberal Arts Building alone covered more than 30 acres and was filled with miles of furnishings, textiles, inventions, and oddities—a cornucopia of consumer goods from zippers to telephones. West of the White City stretched the midway, a jostling mixture of food stalls, amusements, and exhibits from foreign countries. Visitors could circle the fair on a small-scale railroad, or, for 50 cents, they could enjoy two revolutions on George Ferris's giant wheel, the first of its kind, which became, for most visitors, the grand symbol of the fair.

The Columbian Exposition was the United States's unabashed proclamation to the rest of humanity that the young democracy had arrived and was ready to join England and France and Spain as a

The title page of this guidebook indicates the range of women's accomplishments displayed in the Woman's Building, including painting, weaving, and literature.

great world power. President Grover Cleveland laid claim to the nation's new status when he opened the Chicago fair on May 1, 1893:

> Surrounded by the stupendous results of American enterprise and activity . . . [we] stand today in the presence of the oldest nations of the world and point to the great achievement we here exhibit, asking no allowance on the score of youth. . . .
> . . . We have built these splendid edifices, but we have also built the magnificent fabric of a popular government, whose grand proportions are seen throughout the world. . . .

Smallest among the 12 "splendid edifices" of the White City was the Woman's Building. The lengthy struggle to build it—and, indeed, the whole battle to include women in the planning and administration of the fair—were proof that there were persistent inequalities under President Cleveland's "magnificent popular government." (In fact, the women seeking space at the Exposition fared better than 9 million African Americans, whose presence was virtually excluded from the fair, except for displays of handcrafted items in two small exhibits. Few African Americans could be seen attending the fair, though it was open to all who could pay admission, and even black porters and janitors were in short supply.)

Women had begun lobbying for a role in the world's fair as early as 1889, when Congress started to plan the 400th anniversary celebration of Columbus's arrival in the Americas. A coalition of

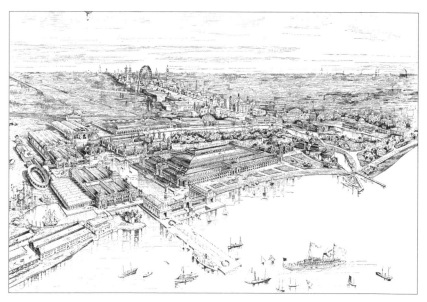

An official guidebook view of the World's Columbian Exposition as seen from Lake Michigan. The Woman's Building is in the upper section of the fairgrounds, at the end of the long midway leading to the ferris wheel.

woman's rights activists and working women demanded exhibit space for women equal to that being given to men, as well as assignments for women on all the governing boards of the fair. An equally determined group of public-spirited socialites and clubwomen, mostly Chicagoans, pressured Congress for a place at the fair that would include a separate women's building.

In April 1890, an act of Congress created the World's Columbian Exposition and awarded the fair site to Chicago. A small amendment inserted at the last moment allowed for the appointment of a separate Board of Lady Managers to handle all business concerning women at the fair. Congress also allotted enough money for the construction of a "Woman's Building." The men in power thus found a way to include the women, though they excluded them from the real centers of decisionmaking and established them in a separate domain. The all-male fair commission also retained veto power and full financial control over all projects .

The 117 members of the Board of Lady Managers included representatives from all the states and territories, as well as a core group of 9 from the host city. Among the members were housewives and professional women, business owners, art patrons, and the wives and widows of mayors and governors. From the western states came a woman mine owner and at least one woman rancher. The women ranged in age from 25 to 70; they were all educated, though not all

President Bertha Honoré Palmer presides over a meeting of the Board of Lady Managers in Chicago in 1891.

college graduates by any means; and they came from the middle and upper classes of society.

The board included both suffragists and anti-suffragists (those who favored or opposed voting rights for women, a heated political issue in the 1890s), but there were no black women, despite concerted pressure for representation from African-American women's organizations. The board as a whole was anxious not to antagonize its white Southern members.

Nor did the Board of Lady Managers contain any working-class women. It was simply assumed, by both the lady managers and the congressmen who appointed them, that an "industrial woman," as they put it, could neither afford the loss of wages nor find the time to attend board meetings. In its final composition the board was socially quite homogeneous, though regionally and politically diverse.

At its first meeting the Board of Lady Managers set up committees and elected its president, Bertha Honoré Palmer, the wife of one of Chicago's wealthiest men. Palmer was a clubwoman and a patron of the arts. She was not a suffragist, preferring, as she would have said, to remain aloof from the seamy world of politics. Nevertheless, she was an able politician, in the broadest sense of the term, and an advocate of women's labor reform. Palmer was a very hard worker, as were the other members of the Board of Lady Managers.

The women were determined that whatever they produced for the fair should be the achievement solely of women. To that end, they found 21-year-old Sophia Hayden, the first woman graduate of the four-year architecture program at the Massachusetts Institute of Technology (MIT). Hayden designed a Classical building, which, although more modest in size than the other structures of the White City, was certainly no poor relation. Like the other buildings, it was constructed of staff, a plaster compound not designed for permanence. The building's columns, friezes, and ornamental roof sculptures were the work of Enid Yandell and Alice Rideout, both 19 years old, and the interior decoration and assembling of exhibits became the responsibility of noted art experts Sara Hallowell and Candace Wheeler. One of two enormous murals that decorated the central rotunda was the work of Mary Cassatt, a young American Impressionist painter who lived in France and was destined to be-

The Woman's Building, designed by Boston architect Sophia Hayden in Italian Renaissance style, faced the north lagoon. All the sculpture was by women.

come the most famous woman artist of her era.

While all this building and decorating was going on, the Board of Lady Managers also had to raise funds for two other buildings: a much-needed Children's Building, which became a large child-care center for fair-going mothers, and a women's dormitory near the fairgrounds, for women who were traveling alone or with children. The dormitory also turned out to be popular with young college women visiting the fair in pairs or small groups.

When their own building was completed, the lady managers filled it with exhibits sent in by auxiliary women's committees in each state. Among the displays were photographs of the Grand Canyon submitted by a woman in Arizona, who had taken them while suspended over the edge in a rope sling with her camera tied to her shoulders. An embroiderer from North Dakota sent a silk opera cloak covered entirely in prairie-chicken feathers. Huge crates of material arrived from foreign countries, including a number of exhibits of women's work that had been denied space in other national and international pavilions.

Decorating the main hall were women's paintings and fine arts, among them some watercolors by England's Queen Victoria. Weaving, fine sewing, intricate lacework, and ceramics were distributed throughout the building. There was an Iowa Corn Kitchen for cooking demonstrations, and a roof garden café that became a popular restaurant for fair goers. The library contained some 4,000 books by women, as well as an enormous compilation of American women's labor statistics, gathered by women on the state boards. The library

Opposite page: This fringed bookmark was one of many souvenirs that the Board of Lady Managers licensed to commercial manufacturers. They also made spoons, fans, and inkstands.

Mary Cassatt's mural "Modern Woman" was installed 48 feet above ground level on the north side of the Woman's Building. The artist was concerned that visitors would not be able to take in sufficient detail from that distance. The bottom picture here shows a detail of the mural.

also contained the first-ever directory of women's organizations in the United States.

In the Organizations Room several dozen women's organizations displayed books, pamphlets, posters, and other paraphernalia of their work. Among the largest of the groups represented were the General Federation of Women's Clubs, the Woman's Christian Temperance Union, the Young Women's Christian Association, the Association of Collegiate Alumnae, the Association of Working Girls' Societies, the Daughters of the American Revolution, and seven missionary societies.

The National American Woman Suffrage Association (NAWSA) had one small booth in the Organizations Room. It was there under the auspices of the National Council of Women, an umbrella organization of more than 50 women's groups. NAWSA had reluctantly agreed to keep a low profile in the Woman's Building, mostly in deference to Bertha Palmer's desire not to antagonize fair goers by including politics in the exhibits.

Despite its size, the NAWSA booth was much visited, and the suffragists were satisfied. Their more resounding successes lay elsewhere, in the women's branch of the World Congress Auxiliary,

Showcases on the ground floor of the Gallery of Honor displayed the work of women from many countries, primarily fine arts and needlework. Other works of art and portraits of notable women lined the walls.

which held a series of conventions and meetings in conjunction with the exposition. The largest and best-attended of all the congresses was the World's Congress of Representative Women, which was held in May 1893. Nearly 500 American and European women speakers, meeting in 81 sessions, spoke on an enormous variety of women's concerns.

Frances Ellen Watkins Harper, a member of the National Council of Women, was one of a handful of well-known black American activists who addressed the congress. Jane Addams, a leader of the settlement house movement, gave a speech, as did Mary Kenney, a bookbinder and union organizer. A session on suffrage featuring Susan B. Anthony and Lucy Stone, two of America's most famous suffragists, was so crowded that one of the younger speakers fainted while the 72-year-old Anthony was briskly clearing a path to the podium.

Susan Anthony was much beloved; her enthusiasm for her cause was notoriously infectious, and she made her audience feel that women had made a great deal of progress in the 45 years that she had been laboring for woman's rights. Always happy to declare even a small victory, she told her audience that the Woman's Building and the women's congresses had given suffrage a big boost. One member of the press declared, "the day of jubilee has come for that plain, tough, staunch, clear-headed and steel-nerved old lady, Miss Susan B. Anthony." Later in the summer, when she was repeatedly swamped

In the Organizations Room, visitors found pamphlets, literature, and memorabilia from several dozen women's clubs and organizations.

by hand-shaking admirers on the fairgrounds, Anthony was asked if all the attention did not tire her. She replied that, yes, it did tire her, "but not half so much as it did 30 years ago to stand alone with no hands to shake at all."

The World's Columbian Exposition came to an end on the last day of October 1893. All the exhibits were packed up and shipped back to their donors. Many of the lovely white buildings burned; others were torn down. Mary Cassatt's mural was lost in the chaos and never recovered. Plans for a Woman's Memorial Building did not materialize, and the members of the Board of Lady Managers and all their state auxiliary helpers went back to their own lives as wives and mothers, reformers, clubwomen, missionaries, teachers, doctors, farmers, suffragists, and socialites.

In the main, the women of the fair had accomplished what they had set out to do: they had convened, without male escort or assistance, from every corner of the country; they had run offices, signed contracts, and paid their workers; they had spent their resources wisely, whereas many subcommittees of the national exposition organization had gone into debt; they had built not one but three buildings; they had mounted a vast international display of women's arts and accomplishments both ancient and modern; and they had run conferences that attracted worldwide attention to a number of women's causes. They had argued about everything; they had been bigoted and exclusionary; they had not changed history or even, as Susan B. Anthony had claimed, made a great deal of progress for woman suffrage. They had, however, made a tremendous statement about the value of women's public activity, a sort of century's-end summation of decades of women's voluntary work and association building, and of their progress in education and the arts.

The 1893 fair was emblematic of much that was relevant in the lives of American women in the years between 1890 and 1920. Many who would be principal players during the next 30 years—both individuals and organizations—were on hand for the exposition; their concerns, conflicts, and ambitions, as well as their accumulated accomplishments, were clearly on display. Equally clearly, the achievements of many women were ignored, their concerns glossed over or downplayed. Like their work and their issues, African-American women, working-class women, and, to a certain extent, recent immigrants were conspicuous by their absence. Exclusivity, racism, and class prejudice were stubborn curses that would continue to blight women's advances in the years to come. Nevertheless, in the Progressive Era many American women—whether together or separately—would find growing personal opportunities. All would face new challenges and continuing struggles to make changes in the American scene.

The inventions room contained the brainchildren of many women, including domestic devices such as carpet dusters and scissors sharpeners. But it was expensive to ship patent models to the fair, and some critics complained that the most important inventions by women were not included.

CHAPTER 2

WOMAN'S WORLD IN 1890

I n 1890, the United States was 114 years old and boasted a population of almost 63 million, nearly half of whom lived in urban areas. The Civil War was 25 years in the past. The country's continental landmass had been mapped in detail from sea to sea and its western acres parceled out among settlers. The frontier was officially declared closed.

Over the next 30 years, an astounding number of social, political, and technological changes were to reshape the nation. Between 1890 and 1910, millions of new immigrants entered the country, most of them from Europe. In 1898 and again in 1917, the United States became involved in foreign wars in which nearly 120,000 Americans lost their lives. By 1912, the last six western territories had joined the Union. In one of these new states, Wyoming, women had had the right to vote in all elections since 1869, a privilege that they held nowhere else in the country. During this period, labor unrest flared up around the country, culminating in dozens of strikes, many of which turned violent when factory owners brought in strikebreakers. Between 1890 and 1920, white Southern vigilante gangs lynched an average of 85 African Americans each year, some of them women and children. In 1893, a crippling four-year depression hit the country, beginning in the very week that the World's Columbian

Women homesteaders in North Dakota maintain an air of formality amid the rough-hewn surroundings of their prairie shack. Western women used decorative curtains and other items to make primitive dwellings cozy and homelike.

Exposition opened. Another depression began in 1907. And, in this same brief, turbulent span of 30 years, a country still becoming accustomed to the potential benefits of the new utilities—gas, electricity, and the telephone—witnessed the invention of the automobile, the airplane, the wireless radio, and the moving picture.

Against this broad background, a generation of American women lived and worked, married, and bore children. Many of them tried to change the world in which they found themselves, either by seeking better work and trying to make a better life for themselves and their families, or by tackling social problems that had arisen in the young country as a result of its rapid growth. Many tried to make a better world for women, who made up more than half the population but did not have full rights as U.S. citizens. The period of years known as the Progressive Era (1890–1920) did not bring women either liberation or full social and political equality, but it was nevertheless an era aptly named, for it was a time when an unprecedented number of women began to find new paths to power and fulfillment.

At the end of the 19th century, when slightly more than half of all working people were still engaged in agriculture and the nation's population was still concentrated mostly in the Eastern states, the

A mother's hard work is evident in the original caption for this photo supplied by a real estate company: "The house is small, but the children are healthy. The stacks are plenty, and the citrons show how gardens flourish in Morton County, North Dakota."

statistically and geographically average American woman would have been a 38- to 40-year-old white farmer's wife with four or five children, living in southwestern Ohio. Like 98 percent of married white women in 1890, this "average" American woman did not work for pay outside of her home. In addition to housekeeping, cooking, and child care, though, she probably performed a great deal of farm labor and may have sold eggs and butter to make a little cash. She may also have been involved in local church work, or a temperance (anti-alcohol) group, or a ladies' auxiliary of the county Grange, an organization that encouraged farmer cooperatives and agitated for farmers' political rights. Our typical mid-continent woman was probably not an immigrant, but she might well have been the offspring of German or Scandinavian immigrants, the groups that had dominated the settlement of the Midwest after the Civil War. Her own daughter, coming of age in the 1890s and educated in a local township school, might have more opportunities than her mother. Unless she married a farmer, or her parents needed her labor at home, she could move to Chicago or some other large city and take up work in a factory, shop, or office.

This picture of the statistically average American woman and her daughter does not tell the whole story. In fact, the typical, if not the average, white American woman in 1890 was just as likely to be a young working-class woman—a Russian-Jewish or Italian garment worker in New York City, a Polish meat packer in Chicago, or an Irish domestic servant in Boston—as she was to be a farmer's wife in Ohio or Nebraska, because immigration was changing the population so rapidly in 1890. The waves of British, Irish, and German immigration had ended in the 1880s. Now the immigrants, who arrived each year in the hundreds of thousands, came mostly from eastern and southern Europe—Russia, Poland, Serbia, Hungary, Greece, and Italy.

Driven out of their native lands, in some cases by ethnic violence and in others by land shortages, population increases, and the loss of village economies to manufacturing, these European men and women came to a country where they had heard they could find both freedom and work. Many newcomers—mostly men—intended to go back rich, and some did. But most immigrants stayed, sending back to Europe for their parents, husbands, wives, and children, or

Italian immigrants, clinging tightly to both children and luggage, arrive at Ellis Island in 1905. The photographer was Lewis Hine.

Lewis Hine also documented the Lower East Side of New York, where horses and people shared the streets of the bustling market district.

for brothers and sisters and cousins.

The 1890s found immigrants squeezed into teeming cities in the Northeast and the Midwest, living largely in ethnic neighborhoods and working in factories or sweatshops—small, privately owned workshops where men and women sewed clothing together piece by piece, usually working long hours at low wages. By 1910, nearly 80 percent of the population of New York City consisted of immigrants and their families.

Even in the most crowded tenement apartments, married women earned money at home by taking in boarders or by sewing or manufacturing small items such as hatboxes or artificial flowers, often employing their young children as assistants. Many of these women remained virtual strangers in their new land, uneducated and unable to speak English, their world limited to the tenement and the few city blocks that made up their ethnic neighborhoods. It was their daughters who went out to work, made friends, learned to speak the language, and contributed their pay packets to the family income.

In large Eastern and Midwestern cities thousands of unmarried women over the age of 16 had jobs outside the home. In 1890, 40 percent of all single white women were in the labor force; 60 percent of single nonwhite women; and 70 percent of single foreign-born women. It was predominantly these young women who would join the growing ranks of the labor movement in the next 30 years to fight for a wide range of rights for working women.

Swelling immigrant populations often pushed Northern middle-class white families into better neighborhoods or out into suburbs, which were connected to the business and shopping districts of the cities by railroads and horse-drawn (later electrified) trams. Women in these suburban families spent their days at home engaged in child care and housework, usually assisted by one or more servants. By the 1890s, middle-class women had learned to relieve the isolation of long days at home with visiting and shopping expeditions and with memberships in women's clubs and civic reform groups. Such groups would experience astounding growth and increasing social and political influence in the decades that followed 1890.

Most white middle-class women still believed in the paramount importance of their function as mothers and homemakers: women were responsible for the health and spiritual well-being of their families, and the family was, as one historian put it, "the principal adornment of Christian civilization and the bedrock upon which society rested." It was a growing impulse to extend this domestic moral guardianship to society as a whole that led so many of these women into the reform movements of the Progressive Era.

Increasingly, the daughters of white middle-class Northern women were well-educated, and they expected to earn high school or boarding school diplomas. It was no longer uncommon for young middle-class women to attend college, either at one of a growing number of women's colleges or at a coeducational university. In 1890, there were more

Jewish immigrants emphasized education in their quest to better their lives. These women formed a literary club that met in Public School 137 on the Lower East Side of New York City.

than 1,000 degree-granting colleges in the United States, and 63 percent of them were open to women. By the turn of the century, 40 percent of all college students in the nation would be women, though that figure represented less than 4 percent of all American women between the ages of 18 and 21.

The picture of women's lives in the South at the turn of the century differed in several significant ways from that of their Northern counterparts. Southern society had been all but destroyed in the Civil War, along with Southern cities and much of the Southern landscape. Recovery had been slow and incomplete, and the South did not share the industrial prosperity of the North. Society was sharply divided along racial lines, and white racism had become steadily worse after Reconstruction ended in the late 1870s. Confined largely to jobs in agriculture, African Americans worked as laborers on vast cotton or tobacco plantations, or as sharecroppers, paying for the fields that they leased from white landowners with a share of their crops. Few black families owned farms of their own.

Although many black women dreamed of a life in which they could devote full time to family cares and household responsibilities, most had to work full days for white landowners or toil in the fields alongside their husbands in order to maintain even a minimum family income. The few jobs available to black women outside agriculture were in domestic service—working for white families—or in laundries, or in segregated mills and cigarette factories. Black

For black women in the rural South, farm work continued to be the primary means of making a living. Many worked as sharecroppers, paying the white landowners a share of the farm's yield in exchange for use of the land.

families made enormous sacrifices to keep their daughters in school, with the expectation that they might become teachers or small-business owners. African-American parents could hope that the next generation of black women might escape sharecropping or working in white men's houses, where they were subject to insult and frequently in danger of sexual assault.

There were, of course, middle-class black families in the South, and even some that were quite well off. Some of the daughters of these families attended all-black colleges or normal schools (teachers' colleges). A very few even went to integrated colleges in the North. It was these women, along with others who had struggled through poverty to educate themselves, who became nurses, doctors, social workers, and teachers, and who founded schools and missionary societies, and initiated black women's social reform efforts in the 1890s.

Not all white Southern women were middle-class. White tenant farmer families and white sharecroppers lived in dismal circumstances resembling those of their black counterparts. White women living outside agricultural areas sometimes sought jobs in cotton mills, though they often found the working conditions poor and the wages low.

Southern white women of the middle and upper classes remained largely homebound, trapped by prewar notions of genteel Southern ladyhood and by white male chivalry, in which men assumed near total control of women's lives in exchange for "protection" of their

An American history class at the Tuskegee Institute, a coeducational black college, in 1902. The writing on the blackboard tells the story of Captain John Smith's rescue by Pocahantas in Jamestown, Virginia. Tuskegee and several other black colleges combined academic subjects with vocational training for all students.

supposed fragility and their sexual purity. State laws discriminated against women, making it especially difficult for them to obtain divorces and keep custody of their children. In one or two states, married women had only limited control over their own property.

Some educated Southern white women had begun to join women's associations well before the 1890s. In these groups—missionary societies, village improvement associations, church groups, temperance leagues—they found identities as reform workers that were acceptable in their restrictive society and that would lead them, after the turn of the century, to more politically charged public activity.

Compared to their Southern counterparts, many Western white women in 1890 found their lives full of opportunity and relative freedom. In the 25 years since the Civil War, cities on the Great Plains had grown like mushrooms. Coal, lead, and silver mines pockmarked the landscape from the hills of Appalachia to the slopes of the Rockies and Sierras. Railroads crisscrossed the entire country, tracing the routes where ox-drawn wagon trains, not 50 years before, had struggled to move pioneer families and their goods a few miles a day. Rapid continental travel was now available to anyone who had the price of a train ticket. By 1890, new farming families from Germany, Scandinavia, Poland, and Bohemia had joined earlier settlers, and farms and ranches blanketed the wide prairies with endless acres of wheat and vast herds of cattle. Independent women ranchers and farmers were by no means uncommon. The Homestead Act of 1862 had enabled the head of any family to claim and work 160 acres of western land, and many single women and widows eagerly took advantage of the opportunity to become landowners.

A number of married women followed their husbands to mining towns in the Rockies, while single women and widows gravitated to growing cities—such as Denver, Salt Lake, San Francisco, and Seattle—where they found work in laundries and other service occupations. Many women ended up working as prostitutes in Western cities. For others, there were opportunities to start small businesses, and some entrepreneurial women owned their own hotels, restaurants, or boardinghouses. Here, as in the East, most women who worked outside the home were domestic servants or teachers, though the Far West had a disproportionately large number of the country's professional women—authors, journalists, doctors, lawyers—who were attracted, perhaps, to a section of the country that still breathed an atmosphere of freedom and adventure.

Western coastal states were especially attractive to Asian immigrants, though the influx of Chinese laborers had slowed to a trickle after the Chinese Exclusion Act became law in 1882. Filipino immigration increased significantly after the Spanish-American War in 1898, and by the end of the 19th century, Japanese immigrants had established substantial communities in California. Although the Chinese and Filipino immigration was at first mostly male, Japanese immigration was more evenly balanced between men and women. The Asian groups tended to remain isolated from the larger, white society, which regarded their different physical characteristics, as well as their languages and customs, with deep suspicion and contempt.

Like women in other immigrant cultures, Asian women remained more isolated and less assimilated than men, remaining homebound or working in restaurants, laundries, or small industries run exclusively by members of their community. Many new brides went straight from the boat to the farms of central California, where they picked fruit and vegetables alongside their husbands by day and cooked meals and cared for their children and living quarters the rest of the time.

Western white expansion in the United States had irreparably disrupted the lives of American Indians. By the 1890s, government authorities had confined nearly all tribes to reservation lands. Whites found Native American culture incomprehensible, unclean, and immoral. The impulse to fence it in was accompanied by the desire to eradicate it through conversion to white, Christian ways. Government agents and missionaries, a number of them women, had been at work among Native Americans of the West for several decades, stressing assimilation and the abandonment of native religions, languages, dress, and sexual customs.

Government programs to convert hunters and gatherers into farmers and herders undermined Native American women's traditional roles in the production of food and clothing, forcing them to abandon the gathering of wild fruits, vegetables, and rushes, and to stop manufacturing clothing from deer and buffalo hides. In many tribes where women had traditionally worked the land, the U.S. government awarded land to male heads of households, thereby destroying the age-old balance of power in Indian families and villages. Women also lost significant political power in tribal councils.

Native American women were able to resist assimilation in a number of ways. Sioux women, for example, maintained their right simply to walk away from unsatisfactory marriages, much to the scandalized horror of white missionaries. Many Indian women also resisted pressure to abandon traditional methods of food preparation. Others learned to exploit the off-reservation marketplace to their advantage. In the 1890s, for example, Navajo women weavers began producing richly patterned rugs for sale in trading posts, providing much-needed cash for a number of Navajo families. In the long run, there was no way Indian women could redeem the losses they had suffered from a century of cultural destruction. Nevertheless, their selective attitudes toward adaptation helped to preserve vital remnants of traditional culture and kept their families alive.

By 1890 it had become clear to many that the 19th-century "Woman Movement" (as it was called) was entering a new phase of broadened aims and growing public acceptance. Poised to enter the 20th century, the movement was endowed with a complex legacy of woman's rights issues and an array of both old and new women's associations that were primed for action.

Blanketmaking was a cooperative venture for Navajo women: the woman at left spins wool, the woman at center weaves on a horizontal loom, the child cards wool, and the woman at right weaves on a belt frame. The photo was taken by Smithsonian Institution ethnographer James Mooney.

Since the first Woman's Rights Convention in Seneca Falls, New York, in 1848, women had been arguing that male dominance and female submission were neither just nor God-given. While agreeing that women were different from men, woman's rights advocates insisted that as human beings women deserved the same natural rights as those enjoyed by men and guaranteed to men by the U.S. Constitution. These rights were to include equal opportunity for education and employment, equal legal protection for everything from property and wages to custody of children, and the right to vote. Other demands included woman's emancipation from restrictive social conventions in dress and manners, for example, and from attitudes that maintained her inferiority.

Gradually, women's advocates expanded their arguments in favor of equality to include a discussion of woman's unique potential for social contribution. They insisted that it was precisely because of woman's special nature—her qualities as a nurturer and moral leader—that she should be given full political and social parity with men, including the right to vote. Because woman differed from man, only she could represent her own interests in the state and community. Furthermore, only if politically empowered, the argument went, could woman make her vital contribution to curing the ills of American society.

Like jugglers keeping several different balls in the air at one time, the leaders of the Woman Movement kept all their somewhat contradictory arguments alive simultaneously, though not without a great deal of contention and confusion. They continued to insist on their natural entitlement to social and political equality with men. But it was their skillful promotion of the public use of women's special talents that won wider acceptance for women's reform efforts during the Progressive Era.

Long before this period, women had begun building associations that brought them together outside their homes. Among the earliest of these were the female moral reform societies, which targeted prostitution—the destroyer of homes and of young women—as a social evil that virtuous women were ideally suited to combat. Also enormously popular were the evangelical church maternal associations, which flourished in the years before the Civil War. The function of these associations was to bring together a public peer

He thinks woman is competent to prepare his son to be a voter—— ——But that she is not competent to vote herself.

This editorial cartoon neatly skewers a notable irony in the "logic" of some opponents of woman suffrage.

group that could support and instruct women in the fulfillment of their moral and spiritual roles within the family.

Like the women in the early moral reform societies and maternal associations, members of the Woman's Christian Temperance Union (WCTU), which was the largest American women's organization of the 19th century, first became engaged in public activity in order to protect their homes—in this case from the social problems caused by alcohol abuse. The WCTU soon expanded its crusade to combat a number of glaring social ills beyond alcoholism, including unsafe working conditions, inadequate schools, and urban decay.

The women's club movement also began to address civic concerns near the end of the 19th century. Clubs were originally organized in the late 1860s as local vehicles for middle-class women to pursue social and literary interests in the company of other women. The movement as a whole enjoyed phenomenal growth, and in 1890 more than 200 local clubs came together in a national federation, which they called the General Federation of Women's Clubs. Like the WCTU, the clubs made it safe for traditional women to engage in political behavior and to see themselves not simply as housewives and mothers but as citizens.

Members of the Women's Christian Temperance Union (WCTU) combine motifs of purity and patriotism in a California parade. Dressed in white—the symbol of purity—they carry the red, white, and blue in support of their cause.

Black American women, unwelcome in the white women's club movement, formed their own federations in the 1890s. The most important of these was the National Association of Colored Women, an organization dedicated to political and educational reform and to improving the lives of black men, women, and children.

Woman suffrage, foremost among the demands of the earliest generation of woman's rights activists, had long been the stepsister of the Woman Movement. Many Americans, both men and women, found this direct demand to share political power with men especially threatening. It challenged conceptions of the "natural" separation of men's and women's spheres. Opponents argued that women, whose strength and solidity were the basis of the family and, hence, of all society, were nevertheless too fragile to become involved in the dirty world of politics. In fact, the suffragists' demand for equal voting rights produced a prolonged storm of opposition because it constituted both a real threat to men's exclusive political control and a perceived threat to cherished ideas about woman's nature and social function.

After the Civil War, suffragists had been bitterly disappointed that abolitionists and Republican congressmen failed to include a woman's suffrage clause in the 15th Amendment to the Constitution, which granted the right to vote to newly emancipated black men. Within a very short time, the suffrage movement had split into two factions. The conservative group, the American Woman Suf-

A training class for kindergarten teachers sponsored by the Colored Women's League. The CWL, founded in Washington, D.C., in the early 1890s, united a number of black women's clubs and reform organizations.

frage Association, was led by Lucy Stone and her husband, Henry Blackwell. The more radical woman's rights advocates, led by Elizabeth Cady Stanton and Susan B. Anthony, formed the National Woman Suffrage Association, dedicating themselves to a broad range of issues, including women's legal rights and labor reform, as well as suffrage. The divided suffrage movement made slow progress except on the local level, where suffrage advocacy did increase during the 1870s and 1880s. In 1890, the two associations merged into the National American Woman Suffrage Association (NAWSA) and elected Elizabeth Cady Stanton as president.

NAWSA was the beneficiary of the decades in which the WCTU, the club movement, and other women's associations had made women's public activity increasingly acceptable. In addition, many women reformers, perceiving that they would be unable to bring about significant change if they lacked the most basic of political rights, soon allied themselves with NAWSA. With its membership on the increase on both state and local levels, NAWSA prepared to focus national discussion of woman's rights on the issue of suffrage and to lead the battle for the vote into the 20th century.

For the new generation of women, these were heady times. By the mid-1890s, the ideals of the Progressive movement had begun to

At a suffrage convention held in Portland, Oregon, in 1905, the dignitaries included Susan B. Anthony (front row, center, with striped bodice) and novelist Charlotte Perkins Gilman.

capture the American imagination, leading concerned men and women to the recognition that their young nation could not, without intervention, overcome the problems that rapid industrialization and urbanization, the rising tide of new immigration, and the excesses of capitalism had brought into being. Progressive leaders directed attention to the problems of American cities—centers of poverty, overcrowding, poor sanitation, and exploitative employment practices—and to the injustices of the nation's economic system. They pointed out that money and property were so badly distributed in the United States that 1 percent of the population owned more than 85 percent of the wealth, while hundreds of thousands lived in poverty.

Books by "muckraking" Progressive journalists, such as Jacob Riis's *How the Other Half Lives* (1890), Ida Tarbell's *History of the Standard Oil Company* (1904), and Upton Sinclair's *The Jungle* (1906), exposed corrupt municipal governments and squalid living conditions among city tenement dwellers, as well as monopolistic business practices in the railroads and oil companies, and filth and danger in the industrial workplace. Farmers and political orators in the new Populist (People's) Party denounced both banks and railroads, which they blamed for agricultural depression and rising farmers'

Social researcher Jacob Riis took this photograph of a New York tenement family. Seven people shared this room and an unventilated bedroom (behind the interior window).

debt. Miners and factory workers went out on strike time and time again to draw attention to their low wages and hazardous working conditions.

In every corner of the land, middle- and working-class Progressives trumpeted the need for social change. They were convinced that society could be transformed if enough people worked to make it happen. For the Progressives, social reform required government intervention on state and local levels, including the passage of regulatory legislation, the funding of government assistance programs, and the creation of government bureaus for social investigation. Reformers also promoted privately run charities and social service organizations, such as settlement houses, which were residential forerunners of the modern community center. In settlement houses, educated, middle-class men and women—mostly women—lived among the urban poor and ran educational and recreational programs for their immigrant neighbors.

Almost all the new public and private avenues of reform would attract women. For working-class women, the Progressive Era would be a chance to focus their energies on the labor movement and the crusade for workers' protection and child labor laws. For middle-class women raised in the traditions of women's voluntary associations,

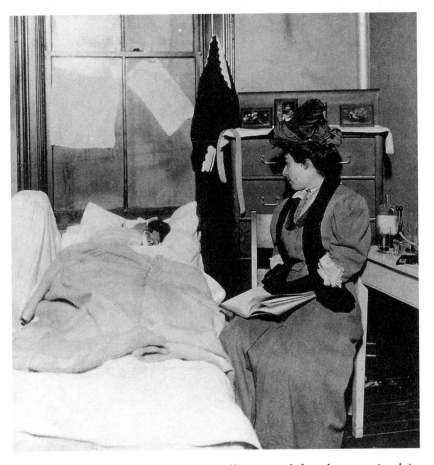

A member of the National Council of Jewish Women reads to a homebound invalid. The NCJW was founded at the Congresses of the World's Columbian Exposition in 1893. It became a multipurpose service organization that assisted immigrants and fostered education among American Jews.

for those educated in women's colleges, and for those trained in grass-roots organizing and lobbying by their long association with suffrage groups or the WCTU, the chance to join the attack on the evils of industrial society was an unprecedented opportunity. The possibilities for personal and social progress seemed endlessly exhilarating. It was an eager and purposeful generation of women that swept out of the house during the 1890s and marched on to the next stage of freedom and responsibility.

CHAPTER 3

WOMEN AT HOME

Although many working- and middle-class women filled their lives with public activity during the years from 1890 to 1920, these women were in a minority. The vast, and mostly silent, majority of American women did not seek changes in gender roles or the existing social order. Many were unable to envision any life other than the one that they currently shared with their families and other members of their class and region. What were the forces and choices that shaped the lives of these women, who kept house for their families, shopped, cooked, raised children, and were largely uninterested in ideas about paid employment, higher education, or voting rights? And what was life like for women who lived in rural isolation, trapped in the unending struggle for daily survival? What about women who could not speak English or those whose most cherished beliefs and customs were alien to the mainstream of American culture? These women, too, are part of the Progressive Era story, for it is their largely unrecorded lives that form the backdrop for the achievements of women who were pioneer educators, suffragists, labor leaders, artists, and rebels. Before we look at the lives and work of activist women, it is important to know how the majority lived and how ideas about women's roles both sustained and limited those lives.

Dr. and Mrs. Love and their children enjoyed rather opulent surroundings in Iowa City about 1895.

For most of the 19th century, Americans had subscribed to the social doctrine of "separate spheres" of activity for men and women. They believed that the urban, industrial work environment—the sphere inhabited by men earning a living—was a corrupt and sullied place. Only men, it was assumed, were strong enough to survive daily contact with the dirty world of commerce and industry.

By contrast, the home, or woman's sphere, was supposed to be a sanctuary from the outside world, where wives, mothers, sisters, and daughters were safely distant from the cash economy. At home, world-weary men might find peace and a renewed sense of honor in the sympathy and love dispensed by the women of their families, women whose lifelong training taught them that piety, purity, and submissiveness were inborn attributes of the female character. These same wives and mothers were also expected to be able to cook, to clean, and to raise both male and female offspring in an atmosphere of religion and morality.

Even the legal system seemed to concur in this conception of woman's nature and work. In an 1873 opinion, the U.S. Supreme Court perfectly described the prevailing idea of womanhood: "The paramount destiny and mission of women are to fulfill the noble and benign offices of wife and mother. This is the law of the Creator."

The doctrine of separate spheres required women to dedicate their lives exclusively to unpaid housework and child care, regardless of their individual personalities, tastes, and abilities. A man might measure his life success in any of a multitude of different professions or crafts, but a woman was considered successful only if she was a good wife, mother, and homemaker.

Catharine Beecher was among the first and most influential of many 19th-century "experts" who attempted to reconcile women to the limitations of the domestic sphere by glorifying their household duties. Beecher was the oldest child in a well-known New England family of preachers, writers, and educators. Her younger sister, Harriet Beecher Stowe, wrote the antislavery epic *Uncle Tom's Cabin* (1852). Catharine Beecher was a teacher, school principal, and author of many popular housekeeping manuals and cookbooks.

Beecher was convinced that woman's maternal and domestic role could be virtually a religious calling. She sought ways to organize homemaking and to develop techniques to help women elevate the status of cleaning, laundry, and cooking from drudgery to a "profession." Beecher envisioned simplified but well-designed homes that middle-class women could run efficiently and with a great deal of personal satisfaction. She also suggested that young girls be trained in homemaking both at home and in school, exactly as their brothers might be trained for their professions.

In the 1890s, the home economists—a group of professional women, largely academics—gave much wider meaning to Catharine Beecher's ideas about professionalizing housework. Led by Ellen Swallow Richards, the first woman professor at MIT, proponents of home economics developed the field into an academic discipline and built whole departments in colleges and universities dedicated to training domestic science teachers. Home economists thought that homemaking was too complex and too important to be left to chance transmission from mother to daughter. Their solution was to train mothers and daughters in the classroom and the chemistry lab in order to teach them how to run their homes according to the most up-to-date scientific knowledge. Characteristic of this new professionalized approach to housework was the application of business and industrial management techniques to the homely tasks of cleaning and cooking. Home economics enlarged the whole topic of housekeeping by bringing it into the public education system and giving it scientific legitimacy. The new discipline helped to transport woman's domestic role into the 20th century and further cemented the relationship between the American woman and her home.

Assumptions about woman's domestic nature and responsibilities were middle-class in origin, but by the end of the 19th century they had come to transcend class boundaries and regional differences. Disseminated across the United States in schoolrooms, sermons, women's magazines, household manuals, and etiquette books, the domestic ideal of American womanhood was almost universally accepted by both men and women. However, like all ideals, this one was never perfectly attainable. Although it represented a goal for many women, to others it was an imposition—someone else's idea of what they ought to be and do.

Even among women whose financial circumstances required them to work for wages in factories or shops, or to perform farm chores, the domestic ideal had tremendous influence. For women whose families

Ellen Swallow Richards was a moving force in the new field of home economics. She served as instructor in sanitary chemistry at MIT from 1884 to 1911. She did mending for MIT's male professors to help win their backing.

Domestic science was a mainstay of the curriculum for women at the Tuskegee Institute. Some graduates might teach in high schools. Others hoped to find jobs running kitchens in black hotels or hospitals.

were burdened by harsh inequalities in the social and economic system, the ideal of ladyhood and domesticity became a distant dream. One widowed young black woman, who told her story to the *Independent* magazine in 1912, explained that the opportunity to run her own home and look after her own children was out of the question. She was a children's nurse who worked for a white family from 14 to 16 hours a day. She was often up in the night with the baby, who was the youngest of the family's four children. The nurse's own children, left in the care of an older sister, were not allowed to visit their mother at her job, so she only saw them by chance in the street, or every other Sunday afternoon, which she had off. She was never allowed to spend the night in her own home. The nurse was paid $10 a month for her work, far from enough to support the children she was not allowed to nurture.

For black domestic servants who did not live in the employer's household, work hours were frequently so long that they, too, were concerned about neglecting their own families. For these women, and for women farm laborers, tobacco factory workers, and many others, the fulfillment of the womanly ideal might have been the opportunity to devote to their own homes and families the same long days of drudgery they were already putting in for white people. However, in rural areas all over the country, black and white families typically mixed work and family life. In the South, in particular,

A black maid in Richmond, Virginia, takes her young white charges to the park. Despite increasing educational opportunities by the turn of the century, many black women in the South were still segregated into domestic work.

where many African Americans worked in agriculture and only low-paying jobs were available, both men and women worked to provide the family income. Most women found ways to share part of the domestic work with other women relatives, and neighboring aunts and grandmothers often helped with child care. The shape of family life for most black Americans, blended as it was with the life of kin and community, was an arrangement dictated by necessity. It might have looked quite different from the middle-class domestic ideal, in which the central image was the full-time mother and homemaker, yet it was a workable alternative.

Middle-class black women had their own set of difficulties in relating to the standards of domesticity set by white society. Mary Church Terrell was a college-educated clubwoman and spirited social activist, married to a black judge in Washington, D.C. Terrell, who had been raised by well-to-do parents to be a respectable lady, daily encountered the effects of racism in her reform efforts on behalf of African-American women. She was also deeply troubled by her own inability to find a well-built, comfortable house in which to raise her children. The Terrells could afford a substantial house in a nice neighborhood, but for years no one would sell to them, simply because they were black.

Like black women, many immigrant women found the reality of their lives at odds with the middle-class American domestic ideal. For some, especially for Asian women arriving on the West Coast around the turn of the 20th century, the important thing was to look like an American lady as quickly as possible. Japanese immigrants, aware that Chinese immigration had been restricted after 1882, were anxious to prove that they could be quickly assimilated into American life. One young bride described her first hour in California: "I was immediately outfitted with Western clothing at Hara's Clothing Store. Because I had to wear a tight corset around my chest, I could not bend forward. I had to have my husband tie my shoe laces. . . . In my case I wore a large hat, a high-necked blouse, a long

This Japanese family, photographed in 1901, is clothed in American style.

skirt, a buckled belt around my waist, high-laced shoes, and of course, for the first time in my life, a brassiere and hip pads."

New clothing was only the first of many adjustments that the Japanese bride would have to make. Wed to a man she had never seen before, because her marriage had been arranged by mail, she would be expected to keep house, raise her children, and work among strangers for the rest of her life.

Other immigrant women, newcomers from eastern and southern Europe, took up housekeeping in large American cities, where they settled with their families by the hundreds of thousands around the turn of the century. They brought along traditional ideas about woman's role that had been shaped by their centuries-old cultures. These ideas echoed middle-class beliefs that woman's primary functions were domestic and maternal, but immigrant women often had notions of housekeeping and ideas about marriage and childrearing that seemed strange to native-born Americans. For example, New

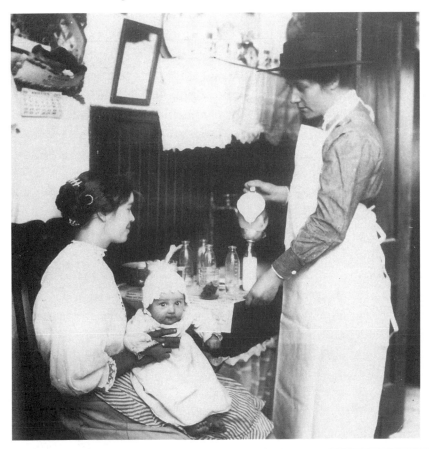

A public health worker shows a Chicago mother how to prepare a bottle for her infant daughter.

York City social workers, raised in a culture that was protective of girls and women, often questioned the wisdom of Jewish mothers who sent young teenage girls out into the work force to help support the family while their brothers were encouraged to remain in school and continue their religious studies.

As for housekeeping itself, even experienced immigrant homemakers could find their adjustment to American life full of painful complexity. A Sicilian woman, recalling her home in the old country, told an interviewer: "We had no blinds, no curtains, and the floors were all made of stone. You have no idea how simple life is over there. Here one must wash [laundry] two or three times a week; over there, once a month." Frequently, immigrant housekeeping methods earned the disapproval of middle-class settlement-house workers and schoolteachers who, though essentially sympathetic with the difficulties of the immigrant families that they were trying to help, thought immigrants' decorating tastes were garish and disapproved of their preferences in dress and diet.

Eager to help turn their parents into Americans, the children of immigrants sometimes grew impatient with old traditions. As far as they were concerned, the crafts and skills their mothers had developed in the Old World had little relevance in America or in the lives of the younger generation. Many immigrant women found cherished needlecraft and other rural domestic industries scorned by their daughters, who could buy the kind of finery they valued very cheaply in department stores.

As the quality of tenement housing slowly improved during the early decades of the 20th century, immigrant women learned to accept not only new housekeeping techniques made possible by the increasing availability of gas, electricity, and running water, but also the changing standard of cleanliness and family care that social reformers and their own Americanized children had been urging upon them for years. At the same time, these women, who had come to the United States from cultures where they produced nearly all the items essential to family survival—food, clothing, farm products—gradually became consumers of domestic goods. In this role they joined their middle-class sisters, adopting an aspect of American life that would grow increasingly important during the 20th century.

In *Breadgivers*, Anzia Yezierska's autobiographical novel of im-

The dress worn by this Italian immigrant mother is decorated with the ornate embroidery of her homeland, but chances were that her daugher would reject such old-world styles in favor of American fashions.

migrant life in New York in 1900, the narrator describes the first stages of the process by which immigrants typically became consumers: "But the more people get the more they want. We no sooner got used to regular towels then we began to want toothbrushes, each for himself. . . . We got the toothbrushes and we began wanting toothpowder to brush our teeth with, instead of ashes. And more and more we wanted more things, and really needed more things the more we got them."

It did not take long for established immigrants to acquire some of the trappings of middle-class homes. Few Americans, whatever their origins, were immune to advertising or the lures of upward social mobility. The national passion for consumption led immigrants to covet and purchase items, unimagined in the old country, that had become necessities in America.

Embraced by the larger American culture and enthusiastically

Magazine advertisments made it clear that a woman's job was to attract and please a man/husband. A neat home—"Glass-towels above, pot-towels below; also graded wash-cloths," the caption read—was the symbol of true affection.

promoted by the experts, the domestic ideal for women was remarkably persistent. Women of various classes and ethnic groups struggled to live up to it. Even as late as the 1920 census, more than 75 percent of all adult women reported that they functioned exclusively as wives, mothers, and housekeepers in their own homes.

The home, however, was not a changeless place. By 1900, the domestic role of women was already beginning to reflect the long-term effects of social and technological changes that had been taking place since the Civil War. Most significantly, women's marital and maternal roles were different from the ones that their grandmothers had experienced in 1850. Marriages themselves were not as permanent as they had been in the past. By 1900 the divorce rate had risen to one in twelve couples; by 1915 the rate was one in nine. Two-thirds of divorces were sought by women, a clear indication that a grow ing number of women were unwilling to accept unsatisfactory marriages and that, increasingly, they had the courage and the means to obtain their independence. The proportion of women choosing never to marry at all had risen from 6 percent (where it had been throughout the 19th century) to 10 percent in the 1890s. Within this new group of women who never married were many educated professionals and others who felt that they could find satisfactory lives, work, and companionship without husbands and children.

Among married white women of childbearing age, the birthrate had dropped 50 percent in the course of a century; it had gone from seven children for each woman in 1800 to three to four children in 1900. Among African-American women the birth rate began to decline dramatically after 1900. By the 1920s about half of all married black women in northern cities were remaining childless, compared to only one-fourth of married white women. The birthrate of immigrant groups also decreased as they became more assimilated into American culture.

All these facts and figures suggest to historians that women were exercising increasing control over marriage and reproduction, that they wanted smaller families, and that they were using available methods of birth control. Because medical advances and improvements in nutrition were also making it possible for women in the early 20th century to live into their 60s and 70s—an increase of 10 years over their 19th-century life expectancy—they could reasonably expect to have a number of years free from child care responsibilities.

Fewer children and more years of life added up to opportunities to engage in work or social life beyond the home and family. For middle-class women, this meant free time to participate in clubs, church groups, and other associations. For working-class women, it might mean increased opportunities for picnics in parks, visits to kin, meetings of mutual aid societies, or, after 1905, an occasional trip to the movies.

Along with the social changes that were opening new vistas of independence for the domesticated American woman came a number of late-19th-century industrial and technological advances. However, change that affected household work was slow and uneven, and at the turn of the century many women in the United States labored over the same kinds of cleaning, laundry, and cooking chores that their grandmothers had performed in the middle of the 19th century.

Utopian schemes for the radical alteration of domestic work, such as those proposed by social critics Edward Bellamy and Charlotte Perkins Gilman, had appealed to both social visionaries and practical reformers, but never seemed to catch on with the general public. Americans simply were not comfortable about exchanging family meals for community kitchens and dining halls, or raising their children in community dormitories. For some Americans "communalism" sounded too much like "communism." For others, the idealized private home—a separate dwelling for each family—was sacred, even though removing some of its most tedious labor would have saved wives and mothers considerable drudgery.

Since most Americans would not accept a domestic revolution, and since it would be several decades before technological progress removed a significant portion of drudgery from housework, constant hard work remained a fact of life for most women. It was especially burdensome for those without domestic servants or household help other than their children.

In her memoir, *Womenfolks* (1983), Shirley Abbott described a typical Sunday morning in the life of her grandmother, Lavisa Loyd, a farmer's wife who was raising 11 children in rural Arkansas in 1914. Loyd rose at dawn, as she did every day, made a trip to the outhouse, carried a pail of water from the well, and then nursed, washed, and dressed her twin infants. She woke the other nine children and sent them scurrying for more water, wood and kindling for the stove, and milk and butter. Together they shook out the feather-bed tickings and made the beds. Some of the children watched the babies while others helped Lavisa cook the breakfast. There were mounds of bacon, eggs, and potatoes to fry, and gravy to be made; three or four dozen biscuits to be cut and baked, and coffee to set boiling. In the half hour after breakfast Lavisa washed, dried, and put away every single dish, cup, and pan, and swept and mopped the floor. She next saw to it that every child was dressed in a freshly ironed shirt or cotton dress and that faces, hands, and ears were scrubbed clean. At 9:00 A.M. Loyd and her husband drove their 11 children to church in the farm wagon pulled by a team of mules.

From Abbott's description of her grandmother's domestic life,

Churning butter was only one of the regular chores for women on the frontier. They also had to milk the cow, feed the chickens, and tend the family's vegetable garden.

Lavisa Loyd might as well have been living in 1874 as in 1914. In rural Arkansas, as in rural Arizona, or Montana, or even in parts of Maine, many people lived as if gas, electricity, telephones, and automobiles had not been invented. On the other hand, city people were already acquainted with these wonders, and with movies and airplanes as well. As a rule, innovation happened more quickly in cities than in rural areas, and new technology was available to the well-to-do many years before it reached the homes of working people. Few of the new home utilities and labor-saving machines were ready for mass consumption before 1920.

Between 1890 and 1920, for example, most American women were still washing household clothing and linen by hand in tubs with corrugated scrubbing boards. In a series of separate operations, each of which required fresh hot water, they boiled the clothes on the stove, rinsed them, blued the whites, and starched nearly everything except work clothes. Every item was wrung out through a hand-cranked roller mangle and hung up to dry, outdoors or indoors, depending on the weather. The next day almost everything, including sheets, had to be ironed, using heavy flatirons that were

Washday in Iowa was a strenuous business. Women scrubbed the clothes in wooden washtubs before running them through a hand-cranked wringer. Washtubs were filled and refilled from wells or hand pumps.

heated on the stove and reheated as they cooled.

All but the wealthiest housewives did some laundry themselves or assisted their domestic servants with the backbreaking labor. Any family who could afford it hired a laundress to come in by the day or take clothing to her own home to wash. By 1910, commercial steam laundries—staffed mostly by women workers—had become big business in cities and large towns, easing the chores of wash day for housewives. In later decades, automatic washing machines would return laundry to the home, making it, once again, the responsibility of the housewife.

The ready-to-wear garment industry had begun to relieve some of women's burdens in home clothing manufacture well before 1890. By 1910 women's clothing was available off the rack in department stores and through catalog sales from Sears Roebuck and other large mail order companies. Clothing came in many styles and all sizes, and it was cheap even by the standards of the day: children's underwear was 12 cents per piece; men's denim overalls sold for 48 cents; and ladies' all-wool, two-piece suits for between $10 and $17. By 1920, most American women were happily buying rather than making their clothing.

Unlike sewing, food preparation remained a great consumer of the housewife's time. Most items had to be made from scratch. Even bread, available at pennies a loaf from commercial bakeries, was baked weekly in many middle-class homes. According to such experts as Marion Harland, author of *Marion Harland's Complete*

This photograph of a woman kneading bread illustrated an issue of Today's Housewife.

Cookbook (1903), the housewife who made her own bread was demonstrating both her love for her family and her mastery of homemaking skills. In fact, almost all home cooking was a challenge, given the uncertain temperament of most turn-of-the-century cookstoves and the culinary tastes of most husbands and children, who expected to be served three cooked meals a day.

Commercially canned goods—fish, meats, soups, and tomatoes—had been available since the Civil War but became cheap enough for mass consumption only after 1890. The invention of the refrigerated railroad car brought to market an expanding variety of fruits and vegetables in all seasons, although goods that had traveled from California and Florida were not always inexpensive. Most housewives had to plan daily purchases of fresh foods, especially meat and dairy products, either at the market or grocery store, or from vendors who sold foods door-to-door in cities and suburbs.

The home icebox, cooled by 100-pound blocks of ice delivered to the home twice weekly, kept perishables from spoiling immediately in warm weather. Because iceboxes were relatively cheap ($5 to $20), all but the poorest families had them. Electric refrigerators did not become widely available until the 1930s, and even in the

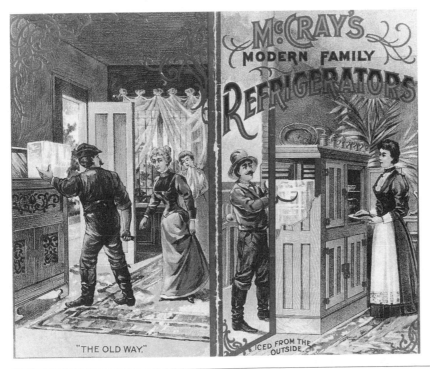

The large, ornate refrigerators in this ad were actually iceboxes and had to be filled every few days with fresh ice delivered by the neighborhood iceman.

1950s some American homes still had iceboxes.

In 1900, nearly all American homes had cast-iron stoves, which had replaced fireplace cooking and heating in all but the most primitive houses. Stoves made cooking much easier and used fuel economically, and their temperature could be more or less controlled through the manipulation of a set of dampers. Many kitchen stoves had attached water-heating and storage reservoirs, which made dish washing and laundry easier than they had been in the days when all water had to be hauled and heated in kettles over the fire.

Most Americans used coal for heating and cooking, though families burned wood in parts of the country where trees were still abundant. Coal and wood smoke left a thin film of grime on furniture and windowsills and embedded itself in carpets and curtains, making housecleaning a repetitive and thankless task. Coal-fired furnaces and central heating systems, which burned more cleanly than small stoves and had been available for decades, were still so expensive in the 1890s that they were found only in the urban homes of affluent people.

By the 1920s, as a result of changes in steel manufacture and new techniques of mass production, costs came down, and central

For years, women had cooked in cast-iron pots on iron hearths. Maintaining the proper temperature and timing was an inexact art.

heating became a standard feature of new houses and apartment buildings. Suburban homeowners also sought ways to install furnaces and hot-air vents or radiators in existing houses. The basement furnace was far from universal in this period, however. Many middle- and working-class folk still had to haul wood from the woodpile or coal from the basement to the stove several times a day.

In the early 1890s, the new gas appliance industry began a massive marketing campaign to get homeowners to use gas for heating, cooking, and lighting. Gas lighting had been a feature of city streets and other public places since before the Civil War. Now there were gas cooking ranges for homes, as well as gas space heaters and furnaces, gas hot-water heaters, gas wall lamps, gas-fired laundry room boilers, and even gas toasters and hair-curling irons. With gas, kitchens would stay cool in summer, and living and sleeping rooms could be warmed rapidly.

Gas ranges, as this 1903 ad demonstrates, allowed women to prepare meals for their families with far less mess than on an open hearth.

In 1896, a promotional pamphlet from a large gas company included a testimonial promising the housewife a kind of kitchen salvation to be obtained by installing a gas stove:

> I looked into my kitchen this morning an hour after breakfast and found it clean, shaded, and cool, although the September heat is intense out-of-doors. As soon as the meals are sent to the table every bit of heat is shut off from range and room. . . . Think of having no coal to bring upstairs; no dampers to regulate (and to break); no ashes to take out; no kindling wood to buy or chop; no fretting because the fire is too low to toast your bread and to broil your steak. . . .

Gas for cooking certainly made a difference. But gas had to be piped into homes, and for a long time it was available only in major metropolitan areas. Although gas was a cleaner fuel than wood or coal, gas lamps did produce soot, and small gas appliances were not portable. By the 1920s, gas was firmly established in urban areas as an excellent fuel for cooking and heating, but it had lost a significant part of its domestic market to the new technological wonder, electricity.

Electric lighting, invented by Thomas Edison and developed by his financial backers in the 1880s, was available in large cities in the 1890s. The industry spawned numerous inventions so that by 1893 many examples of the potential uses of electrical power were on hand to amaze and delight visitors to the Electricity Building at the World's Columbian Exposition in Chicago. Even the most humble of fair goers, those who would be returning home to wood stoves, backyard water pumps, brooms, and galvanized washtubs, could see the future demonstrated in the pavilion's complete model house, which featured electric light and stoves, washing and ironing machines, dishwashers and carpet sweepers, and small appliances such as toasters and plate warmers.

In a remarkably short span of years, the Edison electrical system was in place throughout much of the country. The electrical future became the present, as Americans wired their homes for electricity in ever-increasing numbers. By 1920, 34.7 percent of urban and suburban residences nationwide had electrical wiring. During the next two decades, as manufacturing boomed and prices fell to meet middle-class incomes, people began to acquire motor-driven washing machines and refrigerators in addition to electric light.

Compared to the complexities of the Edison electrical system, the engineering required for basic household plumbing was not a difficult technology. Piped water and flush toilets had been available to the rich since the Civil War. But indoor plumbing and appliances—sinks, bathtubs, and toilets—were not mass-marketed nationally until after the turn of the century. Many rural families continued to rely on a backyard pump or well, or even, in some cases, a nearby stream or pond for all their water needs.

For many city dwellers, water still had to be fetched from an outdoor pump.

Like the hand pump, the outdoor toilet was a common feature of rural life and remained so in some places until after World War II. Major cities and towns, responding to public health concerns about sewage and disease, had installed basic municipal water and waste systems during the 19th century, but these were seldom connected to either the tenements or small single homes of the urban poor until after 1900.

In sophisticated cities like New York and Philadelphia, where hot and cold running water and full bathrooms were becoming standard equipment in most middle-class houses and apartment buildings, the woman whose home was a tenement might find herself hauling all her water for cooking, dishwashing, and laundry from a single cold-water faucet in the hallway, and disposing of it by dumping it out the window, just as her ancestors had done for centuries in the old country. The tenement's single toilet per floor might also be in the hallway, shared by as many as four or five families and numerous paying boarders.

Urban housing improved rapidly in the prosperous years just before and after World War I (rural areas modernized much more slowly). People whose fortunes were on the rise, many of whom were immigrants, found new apartments with electric light, gas cooking stoves, hot and cold running water in both kitchens and bathrooms, and giant basement furnaces that heated whole buildings.

Ironically, the opportunity to improve housekeeping with new sources of energy and new appliances would actually make housework more complex, multiplying some tasks while relieving the burdens of others. The presence in the home of hot running water meant washing and cleaning were easier, but also suggested the need to take more baths or to mop the floor more often. Washing machines made it possible to wash the same clothes more frequently than before. Easily regulated gas or electric ovens meant the housewife could attempt more elaborate cooking and baking than her mother had been able to produce in her day. Despite its heavily advertised promises, the new domestic technology did not actually liberate women from housework. Rather, it served to intensify the personal importance of the home and the woman's role in it by suggesting that her housework could be scientifically perfected.

Modern indoor plumbing fixtures were all the rage in early 20th-century America. They were displayed with great elegance in this St. Louis showroom.

In their early days, telephone companies had to convince consumers that their product was useful. Manufacturers made a particular appeal to women, assuring them that the instrument would give them security and convenience.

"You will send it by special messenger? Thank you."

The Telephone Assists Housewives

THE affairs of the household make the **telephone** a valuable assistant to housewives. It has so many uses in making home management easier and more convenient.

The telephone puts the home within instant reach of all up-to-date stores; with the doctor, lawyer, dentist; with the husband at his place of business; in fact, the telephone keeps the home in touch with everyone who can add to its comfort or offer it protection.

Why not have a telephone in YOUR home?

Just telephone, write or call at our nearest Commercial Office for further information regarding residence telephone service

NEW YORK TELEPHONE CO.

All the domestic experts and professional home economists promoted scientific housekeeping and the consumption of new appliances and energy sources. In magazines and books, on the lecture circuit, and in secondary schools, where domestic science became part of the required curriculum for girls, these authorities encouraged homemakers and potential homemakers to time their tasks, to break household jobs into segments, and to follow strict sanitary guidelines, especially in cleaning bathrooms and kitchens, potential sources of infectious disease. Mothers were instructed to keep infants on strict scientific schedules for eating, sleeping, and playing. Girls learned the chemistry of foods and cooking, reinterpreting recipes and even entire menus according to their caloric values, often with little regard for their taste.

By 1920, housewives had more rules to follow, more goods to purchase and consume, more technological help and fewer domestic servants, and—because they knew more and could do more—an even stronger sense of responsibility for the health and well-being of their families than they had had 30 years before. Some tasks—bread making, clothing manufacture, and (for a time, anyway) laundry—had been moved outside the home, but more elaborate cleaning, cooking, and child care techniques had replaced them. No longer the family's moral guardian, as she had been in the 19th century, the 20th-century housewife had become the guardian of family health and psychological well-being as well as the keeper of the family purse and chief of expenditure. Her title, hours, work load, and "wages" were the same, even if the equipment and the instruction booklet had changed.

In 1920, hardly anybody talked about "woman's sphere" anymore. The new American homemaker had fewer children than her predecessors, more free time, and a more companionable relationship with her husband. Increasingly, married women were entering the paid work force. Indeed, the essential identification of woman with home was in the process of being challenged by women's growing presence in the professions and by their new participation in public life. Broad-ranging role changes, however, lay in the future. For the vast majority of women in 1920, domesticity was still destiny in America.

The Apex vacuum cleaner company tried to flatter women by calling them "managers of the finest industry in human affairs." Like home economists and women's magazines, advertisers frequently sought ways to endow housework with the prestige of professional employment.

CHAPTER 4

WOMEN AT WORK

Marriage, home, and family were universally acknowledged to be the goals of young women in turn-of-the-century America, whatever their backgrounds. In fact, fully 90 percent of all American women could expect to be married at some time in their lives. For most middle- and upper-class women, domesticity would become a full-time occupation. But for working-class women, most of whom spent their adolescent years engaged in some form of wage work, the fact of marriage and motherhood did not necessarily mean that paid labor ceased altogether. Their lives told a different story, one in which earning income was linked to the fulfillment of their roles as wives, mothers, and daughters.

In the majority of immigrant families and for many working-class families of native-born Americans, the standard middle-class pattern, in which an entire family lived on the income of one man, was completely unachievable. The wages paid to a semiskilled working man in 1909, for example—between $12 and $15 a week—were simply not enough to sustain a family. In large cities, rent often took between a quarter and a third of the family income and frequently did not include heat or fuel for the stove. Food, purchased daily to avoid spoilage, was relatively expensive. A chicken cost 25 cents,

Even in the North, work for black women frequently involved cleaning—and generally of white people's homes. There was no new technology to help with floor scrubbing.

and potatoes were 2 cents a pound. Pennies for the newspaper, nickels for carfare, loaves of bread, and cups of coffee added up fast. Many families had bought their furniture on the installment plan, and many belonged to unions or mutual benefit societies. These payments and dues had to be met monthly.

Working-class families adopted a variety of strategies to expand their incomes. In African-American families, where education was prized as a way out of poverty and second-class citizenship, children and teenagers remained in school while their mothers sought work as field hands, domestics, or laundresses. In Northern mill towns, where entire families worked at the textile mill, parents made child care arrangements with neighbors and relatives for the youngest children so that the mothers could work for a share of the family income.

In the large immigrant communities in major cities, especially among Jews and Italians, protective Old World traditions demanded that married women and mothers stay at home and that children,

Many working-class families depended on the wages their children brought home from factories like this one, a South Carolina textile mill photographed by Lewis Hine.

especially daughters, be taken out of school and sent out to work, sometimes as young as 13 or 14 years old. Daughters were expected to hand over their weekly pay packets, unopened, to their mothers. Usually they received back only carfare and lunch money, and perhaps 50 cents spending money, from an entire week's wages of some $6 to $8. The rest was applied to family living expenses.

Married women worked at home to supplement the family income by taking in laundry or garment-making piecework, by rolling cigars, or constructing artificial flowers. Fully 12 percent of American working women were employed in home work, usually making or finishing items for which an outside contractor paid them by the piece.

Perhaps the most common way for married women to augment the family income was by taking in boarders. In immigrant communities all over the country, where men heavily outnumbered women, it was a typical practice for a workingman to board in the home of a fellow immigrant and his family while saving money to bring his

A mother holds her baby on her lap while assembling cigarettes on her kitchen table. It was customary for young children to assist their mothers in such home enterprises.

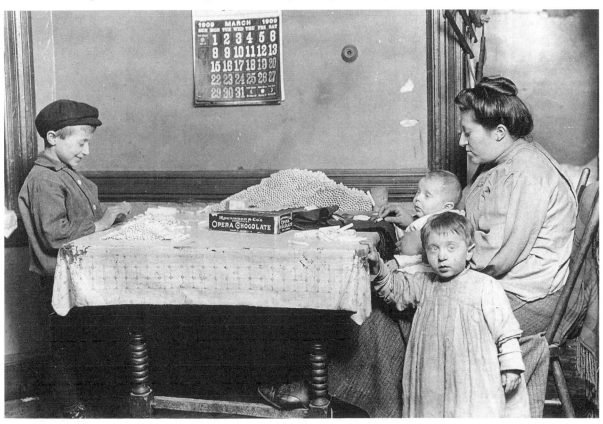

These Slavic immigrant factory workers await their dinner at a New York City boarding house in 1912. Married women often took in boarders to supplement the family income.

own family to America. Women who took in boarders were expected to provide two or three meals a day and clean laundry, as well as a bed—and possibly a room—for the boarder. Many families had several boarders, each paying a weekly fee and often sharing tiny tenement apartments with the landlady's family. Some New England textile communities surveyed in 1909 had an average of 2.4 boarders per family.

While mothers stayed at home and brought in money, their daughters were out working in the industrial world. According to the census of 1900, about 5 million women worked for wages outside the home—approximately one in every five women in the country. By 1920, the nonagricultural female labor force, largely urban-based and white, had swelled to 7.5 million. Most white working women were under 25 years of age, and three-quarters of them were single. For these women, industrial jobs tended to concentrate in the production of textiles, shoes, shirts, and accessories such as hats, gloves, stockings, and collars. They also worked in canning, bottling, and meat-packing factories and in bookbinding and cigar making. Ten percent of America's working women were professionals, mostly teachers, and another 10 percent were clerks and saleswomen.

Nearly a quarter of women workers were African Americans employed in Southern agriculture, in laundry work, or as domestic servants. They were excluded, until the middle of World War I, from all but the most menial of manufacturing jobs—sweeping, scrubbing, and cleaning factory rest rooms—because of their race. Unlike most of their working-class white counterparts, African-American women at the turn of the century could expect to work for wages outside their homes throughout their single and married lives. In Southern cities and towns, widows and grandmothers often took jobs in old age to support themselves and dependent relatives who had been thrown out of work by the unstable labor economy of the South.

By far the largest employment sector for young American women, both black and white, was domestic service. In 1900, one-third of all wage-earning women—nearly 2 million of them—worked either as servants in private homes or as waitresses in hotels and restaurants. The great majority of household servants in the North, Midwest, and West were white immigrant women or their daughters, though native-born white women continued to work as domestic servants in country towns and villages. In the South, white middle-class families almost exclusively employed black women as maids, nurses, cooks, and laundresses.

Because the weekly wages of domestic servants were comparable to those of factory hands, and room and board were free, domestic service gave immigrant women a chance to save money. Among Irish servants it was common to send money back to relatives in Ireland or to pay ship's passage for parents and siblings who wanted to immigrate to America. Women from other immigrant groups—Germans, Scandinavians, and Slavs, for example—went into domestic service because they spoke little or no English and were unqualified for many other jobs. For some new arrivals domestic service provided a chance to learn a little English and become familiar with American culture.

Though some middle-class households employed more than one domestic servant—cooks, nursemaids, laundresses, and handymen were often hired as supplemental help—the most common type of domestic was the general servant, or maid-of-all-work. She labored alone at any and all tasks her employer designated as hers, including all the cleaning and cooking and often the laundry. Fourteen-hour days were not unusual, and few servants had more than two afternoons or one afternoon and one evening off a week. Even with the

The clean surroundings and good food of a middle-class home made the life of a maid apparently more attractive than that of a factory worker. But many young women preferred the independence and higher social status of factory work.

long hours, domestic service was generally thought to be healthy work, partly because a middle-class diet gave servants improved nutrition and partly because the clean, middle-class home in a good neighborhood was considered a morally and physically safe environment for a young woman who had to earn her living.

A typical day for a maid-of-all-work might resemble that described by a Midwestern domestic, Inez Godman, for an article in the *Independent* magazine. Her day started at 6:00 A.M. and ended as late as 10:00 P.M. Struggling with a coal-burning stove, she cooked, served, and washed up the dishes, pots, and pans from three full meals. After making the beds, she dusted, cleaned floors, ran errands, and baked bread, frequently breaking off her work to answer the front and back doors to visitors or tradesmen. If she was lucky, she would get a half hour to sit down in the afternoon, but mending and ironing were always waiting. If there was company, she might be required to stay up late in order to usher the last guest to the door.

For most young women the negative aspects of domestic service—drudgery, loneliness, the lack of personal freedom, and the sense of social inferiority—seriously outweighed the positive ones. Few remained long in any one household, and fewer still saw domestic service as any kind of lifework or career. Even though middle-class housewives kept up a constant demand for maids and cooks, and service jobs were always available, most urban young women preferred to take their chances with industry and commerce, where health hazards and fluctuating wages constituted the price they were willing to pay for after-hours freedom and the right to choose where and with whom they lived, what they ate, and who their friends were.

By 1920, as job opportunities in clerical, sales, and manufacturing work expanded, the proportion of full-time live-in household workers had dropped to less than one-sixth of all wage-earning women. Domestic service did not disappear, but it became, increasingly, and then overwhelmingly, the province of African-American women, who

A black maid, who probably did not "live in," waits on a prosperous family in Topeka, Kansas, around the turn of the century. Families throughout the country depended on the service of African-American women.

performed domestic service in Northern cities just as they had done it all over the South for more than half a century. Except for those employed in caring for very young white children, Southern black domestics had, since Reconstruction, insisted on their right to live away from the job. It was an arrangement that gave them freedom from the constant supervision of the white employer and allowed them to maintain families of their own. When black women began to move to the North during World War I, they replaced white live-in domestic workers who were eager to move on to newly available jobs in industry and business.

In the first decade of the 20th century, women represented at least half of all workers in textile mills and tobacco factories, and in the garment industries they outnumbered men. About a third of all immigrant women who worked found "unskilled" jobs in factories. They tended to congregate in certain industries by region and by ethnic group. Textile mill work in New England, for example, was performed largely by French-Canadian and Polish immigrant families, and both single and married women worked at the looms to supplement the family wage. In New York City, the headquarters of the garment industry, the dominant work force was Italian and Russian Jewish. In large Midwestern cities such as St. Louis, Minneapolis-St. Paul, and Chicago, women from middle-European families—Poles, Czechs, and Bohemians—worked as meat packers and canners.

In Pittsburgh, some 122,000 working women packed crackers

In Southern tobacco factories, black workers were generally restricted to the foulest and worst-paid job: the painstaking chore of pulling the stems from tobacco leaves.

and canned molasses, or worked at simple (and low-paid) "women's" jobs in the steel industry. In California, coastal women canned fish, and others packed fruit and vegetables in the fertile Central Valley farmlands. In the South, textile mills hired white women exclusively, but Southern tobacco-processing plants hired both black and white women, allocating the poorest-paid, dirtiest, and most noxious jobs to the African-American workers. The relatively higher paying jobs, and the clean work, such as rolling cigarettes and operating machinery, were exclusively reserved for white women workers. All over the Northeast, Midwest, and Far West, in major cities and in large towns, white women of almost every ethnic background worked in commercial steam laundries, outnumbering better-paid male laundry workers by a ratio of eight to one. By 1910 the number of women employed in steam laundries had grown astronomically, and there was one laundry worker for every 152 people in the population.

This laundry in San Francisco, owned by a woman, employed both male and female workers. Its windows indicate that it served both male and female customers.

Not only were women's industrial work choices governed in large measure by ethnic clustering and racial segregation, but the occupations employing the most workers were segregated by sex as well. The positions women could get were frequently limited by traditionally conservative ideas about gender. Work deemed appropriate for women tended to be menial or to resemble housework and other traditional women's concerns, such as needlework or food preparation. Women's jobs also paid much less than those of men doing the same or similar kinds of work in the same trade.

The advent of new machinery and new work force efficiency techniques, called scientific management, contributed to the "de-skilling" of labor, either by eliminating tasks formerly done by hand or by breaking the tasks down into ever-smaller segments. In many factories, for example, no worker completed a whole garment or shoe by himself, and no one needed more than a day's training to learn the simple, repetitive work. With all these changes in the technology and management of the factory system, some men did lose jobs to less-skilled women, who would accept cruelly low wages in order to help their families survive. When working men blamed women for taking their jobs or depressing their wages, they failed to see that it was not the fault of women who needed to work, but the fault of an industrial system organized solely for profit.

Few industrial jobs for women held any possibility of advancement, and it was not until after World War I that women became job foremen or floor managers to any appreciable extent. Many jobs, like candy making and bookbinding, were subject to seasonal rushes and slack times; women garment makers often found they worked a 14-hour stretch for three days and then had no work—and no pay— for the rest of the week. Work hours grew shorter, and by 1920, the 54-hour week had become the legal standard in New York and a number of other states.

Although working conditions improved gradually in the first two decades of the 20th century, they remained a source of concern for investigators as well as for workers and union organizers in a number of industries. Dorothy Richardson, a journalist from rural Pennsylvania, described the conditions that she encountered in several New York industries while looking for work in 1903 and 1904. In a cardboard-box factory, where the speed of the work was set by the rapid pace of the machinery, she found her skirt quickly covered with glue, her hands blistered, and her legs and ankles in agony from standing without a break. She was faint from the heat, the noise, and the foul-smelling air—and all of this happened before lunch!

At a subsequent job in a steam laundry, Richardson found the work even more exhausting, the conditions much worse. Her description of the vast workroom suggests an inferno of steam and boiling suds, peopled with oddly clad women "sorters" and "manglers" and what she described as "fifteen half-naked Negro men," who ran back and forth feeding the clean, boiled laundry through the wringers and trucking it on to the next stage. All day long the floor ran with water, soaking the women's feet and long skirts. Richardson's back and arms ached from her job shaking out the linens that were on their way to the giant ironing mangles. By the end of the day she was in such a state of exhaustion that she wandered the streets of the city for hours, not knowing where she was.

In addition to her concerns about working conditions, Richardson also voiced fears about morality in the industrial workplace. The possibility of sexual harassment was certainly present, but for the most part, working "girls," often tightly restricted in their parents' homes, found that the presence of fellow workers made it safe to enjoy the easy camaraderie of the shop floor, even in mixed-gender workrooms.

Conditions were typically primitive in this New York City artificial flower workroom. Boxes are balanced precariously on a shelf over the workers' heads, and there is an unprotected gas jet suspended over the table despite the flammable materials all around the shop.

In the garment industry, the sweatshops of the 1880s and 1890s—small, ill-lit, poorly ventilated, and overcrowded—were gradually being replaced by larger factories. Sometimes working conditions were not much improved by the move to larger premises. The most infamous of all garment industry workplaces was the Triangle Shirtwaist Company on Washington Square in lower Manhattan. The Jewish and Italian women who made shirtwaists—white cotton blouses trimmed with pleats or ruffles—worked long hours for Triangle in the upper floors of an unheated building. Their pay, usually no more than $6 a week, was docked for lateness, for spending two or three minutes too long in the rest room, for talking on the shop floor, and for mistakes in sewing. The air at Triangle was filled with cotton dust, the floor stained with oil from the sewing machines and cluttered with rags. Foremen routinely locked the fire doors to prevent petty pilfering and unscheduled breaks.

On March 25, 1911, a fire broke out on the eighth floor of the Triangle Company's building. With the doors locked on the outside, the workers were trapped in rooms where the oily floors and

This rare photograph documents the tragedy of the Triangle Shirtwaist fire: the bodies of young women who jumped to their deaths lie lifeless on the sidewalk. The police and bystanders are watching for other victims trapped in the upper stories of the flaming building.

lint-filled air soon burst into flames. Those who reached the rusted
fire escapes found the structures crumbled under their weight. Some
women suffocated or were burned to death at their sewing machines;
others jumped from the windows, their hair and clothing in flames.

Hoses and ladders were too short to reach the floors where the
fire was raging, and the firefighters' nets were not strong enough to
hold the weight of the plunging women. Soon the pavement was
littered with charred and broken bodies. Frantic family members,
rushing to Washington Square to see if their loved ones were still
alive, had to fight their way through crowds of onlookers, who stared
at the carnage, horrified and helpless.

In all, 3 men and 143 women and girls died in the fire, making it
one of the worst disasters in industrial history. At a memorial service held in the city's Metropolitan Opera House, city fathers pro-
posing changes in fire laws and equipment were booed by angry
workers. Rose Schneiderman, a young immigrant labor organizer
for the International Ladies Garment Workers Union, came forward
to speak. Her solemn words struck a deep chord with the assembled
workers:

> I would be a traitor to these poor burned bodies if I came here to
> talk good fellowship. We have tried you good people of the pub-
> lic and found you wanting. . . .
>
> This is not the first time girls have been burned alive in the city.
> . . . Every year thousands of us are maimed. The life of men and
> women is so cheap and property is so sacred. . . . it little matters
> if 143 [sic] of us are burned to death. . . .
>
> I know from my own experience it is up to the working people to
> save themselves. The only way they can save themselves is by a
> strong working-class movement.

Rose Schneiderman's words were more than prophetic. The strong
working-class movement was already under way, and women were
militantly involved as they had never been before. Scores of new unions
in dozens of industries would be born and grow stronger in the period leading up to World War I. Their efforts were inspired by the
new generation of immigrant workers, who combined radical traditions they had brought from Europe with a faith in freedom and
possibility that was distinctly American. The new labor leaders, many
of them women, dedicated their lives to the belief that working-class

*Rose Schneiderman went to
work as a cap maker at age 13
and quickly became a leader in
the labor union movement. She
was one of the most eloquent
speakers in the Women's
Trade Union League and in
1928 was elected its president.*

solidarity would transform the existence of the American poor.

For a few years in the 1880s, before it collapsed under its own size and increasing competition from the new American Federation of Labor (AFL), the Knights of Labor had successfully organized hundreds of thousands of skilled and unskilled workers, both men and women, black and white. The AFL, meanwhile, concentrated its energies on organizing unions for skilled male craftsmen. The AFL was not interested in industrial unionism—the organizing of masses of unskilled workers, such as miners or mill workers, by industry rather than by specialized craft. Many Americans, including the AFL leadership, felt that industrial unionism was under the control of revolutionary socialists. They were deeply suspicious of the socialist Industrial Workers of the World, or Wobblies, who were successfully organizing miners and mill workers in the opening years of the 20th century.

The AFL, unlike the Wobblies, ignored African Americans for many years. And, though it did charter a number of women's local unions between 1890 and 1920, it was heavily biased against women workers. The AFL leadership believed that women should be at home and not in the workplace, and feared that women's willingness to accept low wages constituted a threat to male jobs and wage levels. The AFL would be very slow to realize that encouraging divisions between men and women workers only retarded the progress of labor unionism as a whole, for women were in the workplace to stay.

Difficulties with the AFL and the hostility of working men encouraged working women to organize independent, single-sex unions and to seek leaders from among their own ranks. In the Midwest in the 1890s, these efforts enjoyed some success under the leadership of female socialists and union organizers such as Elizabeth Morgan, Lizzie Swank Holmes, and Mary Kenney O'Sullivan. By 1903, the Ladies Federal Labor Union and the Illinois Woman's Alliance had organized some 35,000 women workers in 36 different trades, and they had won substantial gains: Women's wages had risen between 10 percent and 40 percent, and their hours had dropped to 53 per week. Child labor had been almost eradicated, thanks to a push for factory inspection and legislative change, which was a big part of the organizers' strategy.

In this period, working-class women began to form alliances

Left, members of the Women's Trade Union League demonstrate in midtown Manhattan. The membership included leading members of society who supported the cause of working women. The league's seal embodied the domestic basis for labor reform.

with middle-class women reformers such as Jane Addams, who were concerned about the condition of women and children working in industry. In 1903, Mary Kenney O'Sullivan, in concert with William English Walling, a socialist intellectual and settlement house worker, and Leonora O'Reilly, a former garment worker and schoolteacher, established the Women's Trade Union League (WTUL), with offices in Boston, New York, and Chicago. The AFL endorsed the league, but did not give it much financial support.

Middle-class women reformers, social activists, and a few wealthy philanthropists joined the WTUL. Some, like Margaret Dreier Robins, league president after 1907, and her sister, Mary Dreier, who was president of the New York branch, dedicated many years of their lives to the WTUL. Working women such as Rose Schneiderman, who became president of the league in 1927, and Leonora O'Reilly, its finest orator, labored throughout their lives for the league and related women's causes, never marrying, and never retiring, except in their final illnesses.

"I thought, as a young girl, that I would get married, too," wrote Mary Anderson, a Chicago shoe worker and league member who became, in 1920, the first director of the Women's Bureau of the U.S. Department of Labor, "but somewhere I lost myself in my work and never felt that marriage would give me the security I wanted. I thought that through the trade union movement we working women could get better conditions and security of mind."

Within the WTUL, working-class women and affluent women

Mary Kenney O'Sullivan, a bindery worker and mother of three, was the first woman general organizer of the American Federation of Labor. She became the founding secretary of the WTUL.

discovered they shared common disabilities related to gender: political powerlessness, limited options for jobs or careers, and family claims upon their time and attention. However, the league motto, "The eight hour day; a living wage; to guard the home," made it clear to any doubters that this alliance dedicated to working women did not intend to threaten the sacred precincts of domesticity or woman's traditional role. It was also clear from the very beginning that the goals of the WTUL would include both trade union organization for women and the integration of working women's concerns into programs for women's rights. Through the WTUL, working women were called upon to support the fight for woman suffrage.

Despite a number of points of disagreement, and the failure of some of the middle-class "allies" to understand working women's backgrounds and aims, the WTUL was a highly effective alliance between middle- and upper-class women and those of the working class. In its support of a massive strike by New York's garment industry workers in 1909, the WTUL was successful not only in winning support for the workers but also in organizing the complex strike shifts and tactics of thousands of women picketers. The league initiated a heavy leafleting campaign, and it publicized the strikers' wage and hour demands, as well as descriptions of their miserable working conditions, in the pages of its magazine, *Life and Labor.* WTUL officers put up bail for some of the jailed strikers, and several of the league's upper-class "allies" joined picket lines and were arrested along with working women picketers. These arrests delighted the press, which brought the plight of striking workers to public attention in an unprecedented array of stories and articles.

The strike ended in February 1910, with many of the workers' demands met. It was clear that the real heroines had been the young women picketers, who, though harassed, beaten, and repeatedly jailed, had stuck it out on the picket line through the worst days of a bitterly cold winter. Nevertheless, the workers owed much of their success to the organizational talents of the WTUL.

The WTUL continued to participate in labor actions around the country, though, in the second decade of the 20th century, it began to turn much of its attention to suffrage, to lobbying for legislation to protect women and children in the workplace, and to training women labor leaders.

Garment workers parade defiantly in Chicago in 1910. Neither police brutality nor the threat of job loss, hunger, and homelessness discouraged them. Gradually, the small group of women strikers grew stronger and received support from the men's unions.

During a famous strike of textile mill workers in Lawrence, Massachusetts, in the winter of 1912–13, the WTUL took a backseat, unwilling to associate itself with the radical Industrial Workers of the World (Wobblies), who were organizing the strike. The Wobblies brought in a fiery young orator and organizer, Elizabeth Gurley Flynn, who was an inspiration to the militant working women at Lawrence. Provoking their own arrests and refusing bail, the women risked their lives as well as their livings in confrontations with police and militia sent in to break up the strike.

A group of mothers was attacked and beaten in the Lawrence railroad station as they waited to send their malnourished children to stay with sympathetic families in New York. Two pregnant Italian women, leading a march of picketers, miscarried after they were attacked by troops in the city streets. A band of women picketers captured a policeman and attempted to throw him in the icy river. Finally, after eight weeks of violence on both sides, the mill owners capitulated, and the Lawrence strike was settled—a great victory for the striking workers and a boon to mill workers all over New England.

One of the longest-running labor crusades on record involved women steam-laundry workers in California. In a series of actions begun in 1900, women secretly organized the industry in San Francisco, winning the right to live out (they had been required to live in company boardinghouses), as well as a wage increase, nine paid holidays a year, and a number of other concessions. That took six years. In the next six years, the union women won an eight-hour day, a 30 percent wage increase, including overtime pay, and the installation of modern safety measures in all the plants. By 1912 they had become one of the few unions in such a low-wage, unskilled industry to last so long and accomplish so much.

While white women and their unions were engaged in labor battles all over the country, turn-of-the-century union organization tended to touch African-American women peripherally, if at all. In the few industrial occupations open to them, black women continued to be paid about half of what white women earned, and no attempts were made to organize black home workers or domestics, though there had been sporadic attempts by black laundresses to organize and strike in Southern cities in the late 19th century. Southern AFL affiliates did not include black men or women, and even unions that did organize black men tended to keep them in separate all-black locals. In Richmond, Virginia, some 367 black men and women tobacco workers successfully maintained a local organization of the Tobacco Workers International Union, but most black women's labor actions in the South consisted of offering support services to black men involved in strikes or walkouts.

In both the South and the North, black women were sometimes played off against whites: They were offered jobs as scabs (replacement workers) when white women workers went on strike. If they took the jobs, black women usually found that they were fired the minute white women came back to work.

Beyond factory work for women in turn-of-the-century America lay the newly expanding field of white-collar work. The rapid evolution and tremendous growth of the white-collar sector became the most dramatic aspect of change in working women's opportunities in the entire 30-year period between 1890 and 1920. Like their sisters in industrial work, white-collar women found that, wherever they worked, their pay was considerably less than that of men doing the same jobs. Partly as a result of pay discrepancies, some white-collar jobs became "feminized" over time, as companies replaced relatively expensive male employees with a lower-paid all-woman work force.

Women flocked to white-collar work, which carried status and, except for salesclerking, was better paid than factory labor. By 1910, more than 700,000 women worked as trained nurses and school-teachers (77 percent of all teachers were women). Another 475,000 women were salesclerks, and nearly 600,000 worked in offices. More than 88,000 women were employed as telephone operators, an increase of 475 percent from 1900. By 1917 this occupation had become so completely feminized that women accounted for 99 percent of all switchboard operators in the United States.

Before 1917, white-collar work was almost exclusively reserved for native-born white women. Immigrants, even second-generation daughters of immigrants who spoke with an accent or had noticeably "foreign" or Jewish names, usually found it impossible to get

In 1911, the telephone operators and their supervisors at Southwestern Bell were all women. This trend was typical around the country. The Bell company insisted that the operator deliver "service with a smile," even though she was never seen by the caller.

sales or office jobs. Black women knew that discriminatory hiring practices in both the North and the South made it useless for them even to apply for white-collar office or clerical work in any but black-owned businesses. Increasingly, and mostly in the South, black women were hired to teach black children. By 1910, 22,547 of the nation's 29,772 black teachers were female. Similarly, black women entered nursing in growing numbers around 1900, after the founding of a number of black nursing schools in the 1890s. Black nurses worked in the black community and as private nurses; they were denied jobs in white hospitals and in the Army Nurse Corps and the Red Cross. Excluded from membership in the American Nurses Association, they formed their own group in 1908—the National Association of Colored Graduate Nurses.

White women who worked in offices occupied an increasing number of specialized positions as typists, stenographers, shipping and receiving clerks, bookkeepers, cashiers, accountants, or office-

The boss of this mushroom factory in Missouri employed a woman to work as a secretary in his office.

machine workers. Their jobs had come with the growth of business and industry and technological advances in business machinery. At the same time that the demand for office staff skyrocketed, the spread of public school education, especially high school training, meant that a growing supply of women was available for office work. By 1915, approximately 50 percent of all office workers, and nearly 85 percent of all typists and stenographers, were women.

Rather than replacing male office workers altogether, women were moving into new jobs created by the specialization of clerical tasks, jobs that had less overall responsibility than those of male office workers and paid much less, but were still highly desirable. Office work was clean and largely sedentary. Therefore it was "genteel," and in terms of status it ranked just below professional work for women. For young working-class women who finished high school, the move into office work was a chance to bridge the gap into the middle class, with the possibility of making new friends or an advantageous marriage.

Sometimes working-class parents had difficulty adjusting to the change in a daughter's status that came with her white-collar job and her desire to be treated as a valuable salaried "professional." Mothers who felt themselves burdened with housework, as they often were, sometimes exacted a full evening's domestic chores from a woman who had worked a nine-hour day at the office, just as they would from a daughter who worked in a factory. Housework was so strongly identified with the female gender that mothers expected help from daughters that they would never have asked from sons or husbands, even when those daughters were contributing a large portion of the family income.

Women's wage work, whether "white" or "blue" collar, domestic service, industrial labor, or home sewing, was an integral part of family life for many Americans in the early years of the 20th century. To working mothers, sisters, and daughters, supporting the family was part of caring for it, just as much as the middle-class woman's single-minded preoccupation with homemaking demonstrated her own adherence to a womanly role and her love for her family.

CHAPTER 5

WOMEN IN PUBLIC LIFE

B y seeking to improve their own lives, to gain better wages and working conditions through union agitation, or to move out of factory labor altogether into white-collar work, working-class women were helping to expand opportunities for women and improve health and living conditions—and future prospects—for city dwellers and industrial workers and their children. Educated middle-class women and women professionals were also seeking better opportunities for women, among a wide variety of social reforms. Frequently they were assisted in their efforts by wealthy women who wanted the personal public involvement that charity work and philanthropy could not bring them. These upper-class or elite women had more money and leisure than their middle-class sisters but shared a common cultural background and reformist tendencies.

Both middle-class and elite women came to the Progressive years, between 1890 and 1920, from a history of involvement with women's associations of the 1870s and 1880s: the women's foreign mission crusade, the women's club movement, the Woman's Christian Temperance Union (WCTU), the Young Women's Christian Association (YWCA), and others. These movements were characterized by their allegiance to the 19th-century concept of separate spheres and the

The front page of The Suffragist, *the magazine of the National Woman's Party, for November 22, 1913. It graphically demonstrates the appeal to Congress for the woman suffrage amendment.*

domestic ideal: their members believed that woman's primary function was motherhood and homemaking. By the mid-1890s, however, women's associations had extended the borders of woman's sphere to include involvement in many outside concerns. They insisted that women were not only uniquely fitted to take a public role in reforming society, but were morally obligated to do so.

The new generation of women reformers, whose immediate predecessors had attacked public evils that threatened the home—child labor, prostitution, alcoholism, and poor education—began to embrace a broader range of projects in the 1890s. Claiming that their reform activities constituted a form of "municipal housekeeping," women's organizations seized the opportunity to tackle a variety of urban, industrial problems. In many ways it was the moral and political issues that concerned women that shaped the aims of all Progressives, male and female, as well as providing the momentum for Progressive reform programs and much of the volunteer labor.

Women's associations, both old and new, experienced tremendous growth throughout the Progressive period. By the first decade of the 20th century, the foreign mission crusade had grown to astonishing proportions, with nearly three-quarters of a million members enrolled in local church auxiliaries all over the country. Foreign missionary work—the worldwide endeavor to convert unbelievers to Christianity—was organized independently by each of the major American Protestant denominations.

The 1895 missionary training class at Spelman Seminary in Atlanta. This black women's college in Atlanta had an all-female faculty. Women trained in missionary work expected to preach the gospel in remote parts of Africa and Asia.

Missionary auxiliaries reflected middle-class interest in domesticity, marriage, and motherhood, while focusing on the lives of women in those distant lands that Americans saw as most backward and primitive. Local auxiliaries met weekly to study reports from women missionaries in Africa, Asia, or the Pacific islands. Contrasting these reports with their own lives of relative freedom and protection, middle-class Christian women deplored foreign customs that compelled women to live in harems or other polygamous marriage arrangements, forced them into marriage as children, or subjected them to ancient cultural rituals such as nose piercing or foot binding.

Missionary enterprises connected American women to the rest of the world and also confirmed their sense of American cultural superiority. The women's enthusiasm provided public support not only for missionary work in other countries, but also for the growth of American imperialism during the years in which the United States first joined other Western military powers in the conquest of weaker nations and the attempt to westernize their societies.

Like the foreign mission crusade, the women's club movement was expanding rapidly in turn-of-the-century America. The General Federation of Women's Clubs (GFWC), founded in 1890 with about 20,000 members in some 200 local clubs, could claim to represent nearly 1 million women by 1910. For a majority of women's clubs, the formation of the GFWC coincided with a change in emphasis from self-culture and amusement to service and reform. Progressive Era clubwomen set up libraries, university extension courses, trade schools, and home economics classes for girls. They raised money for city parks and playgrounds. They lobbied state legislatures and city councils for clean water and better disposal of refuse and for laws to eliminate sweatshop abuses and provide fire inspection for tenement houses. Clubs concerned themselves with the creation of a juvenile court system and joined the fight for federal public health legislation such as the Pure Food and Drug Act of 1906.

Before the turn of the century, the largest organization of American women was unquestionably the Woman's Christian Temperance Union. The WCTU drew members from every region of the country and from every social class, although middle-class, white Protestant women predominated, as they did in the women's club movement. The Union's family-centered philosophy and its emphasis on women's right to participate in public affairs that affected the welfare of homes and families made it a "safe" organization for women to join. Its motto was "For God and Home and Native Land"; its badge was a bow of white ribbon, symbolizing the purity of the home; and its rallying cry was "Home Protection." The temperance reform movement gave women a way to speak out about domestic violence, and it helped to secure passage of legislation that improved women's legal rights to property, child custody, and divorce from abusive spouses.

By the early 1890s, the WCTU had 150,000 members, and, through its overseas missions, claimed millions worldwide by the turn of the century. In Chicago, the WCTU had its own office building, called the Woman's Temple, ran its own publishing company, and operated a medical center. All the work was done by women, and women held all the union's executive positions.

Under the 20-year leadership of Frances Willard, the national union's energetic and imaginative president, the WCTU took on an ever-increasing array of projects that led it far beyond its original commitment to the prohibition of alcohol. The WCTU was organized into nearly 40 departments, each with its own superintendent, and this structure was repeated in the local chapters. Dealing with areas as diverse as labor reform, health and hygiene, social purity, peace and arbitration, prison reform, and education, women learned the techniques of public involvement and political action: lobbying, organization, canvassing, and public relations. As early as 1882, the WCTU endorsed the ballot for women as a "weapon for the protection of the home." The suffrage department became increasingly

The WCTU on wheels, in a 1908 Chicago parade.

active and important as the years went by.

The WCTU was particularly important to Southern white women, who saw it as a respectable way to become publicly active and to escape some of the constraints of their protected lives. To women like Belle Kearney and Sallie Southall Cotten, who later became leaders in Southern reform movements, the WCTU was, as Kearney said, the "generous liberator, the joyous iconoclast, the discoverer, the developer of Southern women." Membership in this large national organization also helped to put isolated Southern women in touch with their counterparts in the North, facilitating the exchange of ideas and, eventually, the entry of Southern white women into the suffrage movement.

Although Southern black women were excluded from white chapters of the WCTU, there were some separate chapters for black women in the South, as well as a number of segregated Northern chapters. Frances Ellen Watkins Harper served as the only African American on the WCTU's executive committee and was frequently critical of the racism of the organization's members, though she was a firm believer in the need for temperance among black Americans.

Temperance was only one of many issues that attracted the attention of black women activists. The antilynching campaign of African-American journalist Ida B. Wells in the 1890s was one of the most dramatic episodes of the black women's reform movement. Lynching, or mob murder of black men (and some black women and teenagers), had become a regular feature of the post-Reconstruction South. It was used as a tactic of terror and intimidation, and black men who had done well in business or other enterprises and were beginning to have influence in the community were often the targets of lynch mobs. With the tacit consent and all the power of white Southern society behind them, mob members had little need to justify their acts of violence against black men, but they frequently claimed that a white woman had been sexually assaulted by the lynching victim.

The 1892 Memphis, Tennessee, lynching of Thomas Moss, a black grocery store owner, along with his two associates, was directly related to white jealousy of their business success. On a Saturday night in March, an angry white mob attacked the grocery store. Three of the attackers were shot by black men defending the store,

Ida B. Wells, journalist, suffragist, and social reformer, is perhaps best remembered for the antilynching cruade she launched in the 1890s.

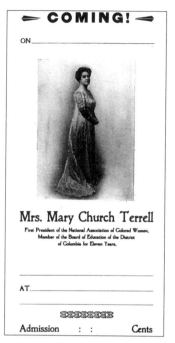

— COMING! —

ON

Mrs. Mary Church Terrell

First President of the National Association of Colored Women,
Member of the Board of Education of the District
of Columbia for Eleven Years,

AT

Admission   :   :   Cents

Mary Church Terrell used this all-purpose flyer to announce her varied speaking engagements. She worked tirelessly for a number of causes, including the establishment of kindergartens and daycare centers for black children, anti-discrimination legislation, and woman suffrage.

and Moss and his partners were arrested and jailed. Kidnapped from jail by the mob, all three were murdered on the railroad heading out of town. Moss left a little girl and a pregnant wife. He also left two very angry friends: Mary Church Terrell and Ida B. Wells.

Memphis-born Terrell, a childhood friend of Thomas Moss, was the college-educated wife of a judge in Washington, D.C. She herself was an educator and would soon become a nationally prominent clubwoman and reformer. After the lynching, she and the revered abolitionist leader Frederick Douglass quickly arranged an audience with President Benjamin Harrison, imploring him to publicly condemn lynching. Harrison did nothing, but Terrell, horrified by this latest evidence of the worsening condition of black Americans, embarked on a life of activism to help her race.

Ida B. Wells was orphaned at 16 and left in charge of five younger brothers and sisters. She rose to the task, earning a meager living as a schoolteacher and sacrificing her own education to provide for her family. By 1892 she had become a journalist and part owner of the *Memphis Free Speech*, a black newspaper. Outraged by the murder of Thomas Moss, she began a series of antilynching articles that were published in the *Free Speech* and other papers and magazines around the country. She also launched an investigation of white mob violence throughout the South, researching 728 lynchings that had taken place in the preceding decade. A segment of her study was later published as *A Red Record* (1895). What Wells discovered, among many other things, was that not only had the alleged rapes hardly ever taken place but that fewer than a third of all the murdered men had even been accused of assaulting white women. Most had been charged with crimes like "making threats," or "quarrelling with whites," or (amazingly) "race-prejudice."

While Wells was lecturing in Philadelphia, the *Free Speech* offices were looted and burned, and her partners fled for their lives. Warned that she would be hanged from a lamppost if she returned to Memphis, Wells knew that she could never go home again. She waged her antilynching campaign in the North, winning support from blacks and whites alike through her lectures and writings. Although lynching would not be fully eradicated for several decades, Wells's campaign had undermined the stereotype of the sexually violent black male. Her intelligence and personal integrity also encouraged many white Americans to question their racist assumptions about the supposed laziness and immorality of black women. She inspired many black women to take action against racial injustice.

For many women of the established black middle class, the response to instances of rising racism in the 1890s was to join the black women's club movement. The movement's growth in the 1890s paralleled the development of the federated club movement of white women at the end of the 19th century. Few black clubs were dedicated to culture, however. From their very beginnings, most black women's clubs were more radical and more activist than their white counterparts. Although the clubwomen were mostly middle-class and educated, their concerns were for the race as a whole and for the elevation of all black women, regardless of class. Their practical efforts were concentrated in education, health, housing, domestic training, and prison reform.

The slogan of the movement, "Lifting As We Climb," reflected the clubwomen's recognition that, although they were themselves privileged, their own survival and advancement, both as women and as African Americans, depended on helping their less fortunate sisters. They knew that all black women were judged by the poorest and most disadvantaged of their sisters. They also knew that all black women were victims of the prevailing stereotype of black female immorality, a relic of the days of slavery when African-American women were at the mercy of white owners' sexual demands. No matter how ladylike her manners, how educated her speech, or how elegant her dress, in many parts of the country a black woman would be treated like a prostitute by contemptuous whites. She might be refused admission to restaurants and hotels, restricted to the second-class smoking car on trains, or arrested without cause "on suspicion of soliciting." Challenging decades of racist public opinion and discriminatory practices became a key part of the black woman's movement.

In 1895, under the leadership of Fannie Barrier Williams and Josephine St. Pierre Ruffin, some 36 women's clubs from 12 states formed the National Federation of Afro-American Women. They elected Margaret Murray Washington, the wife of the influential black educator Booker T. Washington, as the federation president. That same year, in Washington, D.C., Mary Church Terrell was organiz-

The logo of the NACWC was a literal interpretation of its motto, "Lifting As We Climb." It embodied the group's philosophy of self-help and racial unity.

ing women's clubs into the National League of Colored Women. In 1896, the federation and the league united to form the National Association of Colored Women (NACW), with Terrell as its president. The NACW became the most powerful African-American women's organization in the country—a training ground for leaders, educators, and reformers, for political action on behalf of black women and men, and a springboard for the black woman suffrage movement, which was organized by state and local clubs. On the eve of World War I, the NACW had 50,000 active members. A number of its programs were used as models by two new civil rights organizations founded in 1909 and 1910: the National Association for the Advancement of Colored People (NAACP) and the National Urban League.

Women's reform activities of the Progressive Era owed much to powerful associations like the WCTU and to the women's club movements. Reform was also linked to the advances in women's higher education that had taken place since the 1870s, producing a generation of college-educated women possessed of a desire to help and a need to find meaningful work. By 1890, the Eastern women's colleges, Wellesley, Vassar, and Smith, had been in operation for a number

Members of the National Federation of Afro-American Women, a predecessor of the NACW, at their 1895 convention.

of years, and they soon were joined by upgraded girls' academies like Mt. Holyoke in Massachusetts and Rockford Seminary in Illinois. During the 1890s, under its dynamic woman president, M. Carey Thomas, Bryn Mawr College in Pennsylvania obtained a reputation for academic rigor that was equal to that of any men's college. In the West and the Midwest, women had gained increased entry to state universities after the Civil War, though many institutions at first offered only teacher training for women. And in the South, where coeducation was still unpopular, normal colleges (teacher training schools), segregated by race, continued to be most of what was available for both black and white women.

There were about 100 colleges for African Americans in 1900, and a few integrated colleges, such as Oberlin in Ohio. In 1904, with nothing but her fierce determination, $5, and a piece of land that had been a garbage dump, Mary McLeod Bethune founded the school that would become Bethune-Cookman College, a highly respected African-American college in Daytona, Florida.

Astronomer Elizabeth Bardwell (right) works in the observatory of Mount Holyoke College. Construction of the 1881 structure added up-to-date science laboratories to what was originally a seminary.

Although the overall proportion of American women who attended college was very small—7.6 percent of all women aged 18 to 21 in 1920—the increase in attendance was significant: by 1920 women made up nearly 50 percent of all enrolled college students.

It was mostly middle-class women, the daughters of professional men and businessmen, who went to college. Upper-class white American women tended to be educated at home, later traveling in Europe to expand their knowledge of Western art and culture. After they made their social "debuts," sometime between the ages of 18 and 21, they lived a life of leisure, waiting to make good marriages. Eleanor Roosevelt, the niece of President Theodore Roosevelt and later the wife of President Franklin Roosevelt, always regretted the rigid social rules that had denied her a college education.

Considering its middle-class clientele, college was expensive: tuition, room, and board at Wellesley in 1906, with pocket money and books, never cost less than $350 annually. At the University of California at Berkeley, students spent between $90 and $495 a year. In an era in which annual middle-class family incomes ranged from $1,000 to $3,000, college for daughters was often out of the question. Scholarships were still rare. As time went by, it became increasingly respectable for a young woman to work her way through college.

Marion Talbot, head of the department of household administration at the University of Chicago, saw the field of home economics as a way to move academic women into the sciences. Talbot's sometime collaborator, the feisty lawyer and reformer Sophonisba Breckinridge (right), told an interviewer: "I would rather have a good fight any afternoon, even if I get beaten, than go to a party any time."

After graduation, many women progressed to good jobs as teachers, accountants, private secretaries, librarians, or journalists. Others sought advanced study in science and liberal arts, training that would lead to professional careers in medicine and academia. Women college graduates who went to work tended to marry later than their non-college-educated counterparts. More than half of college-educated women with full-time professional careers never married at all, instead finding their fulfillment in work, collegiality, travel, and good times spent with other single women.

For women graduates without the prospect of marriage or any specially chosen career, or for those whose tradition-minded families wanted them to come home, the possibility of a future of aimless leisure and financial dependence loomed unpleasantly. It was women such as these, women looking for a way to put to use the gifts education had given them, who started the settlement-house movement, an urban reform that attempted to help immigrant families make better lives for themselves amid the bewildering complexities of America's industrial cities. The settlement-house movement became the best known of all Progressive Era reforms.

For more than 40 years, Jane Addams was the acknowledged leader of the settlement-house movement. She became the most famous American Progressive of her day, and her work for immigrants and the poor, for urban reform, and for peace earned her an international reputation. Born into a well-to-do Midwestern family, Addams had graduated from Rockford Seminary in Illinois in 1881. She intended to go to medical school, but a prolonged illness made that impossible. She spent nearly eight years battling invalidism and living in the homes of her married brothers and sisters, where she functioned as spinster aunt and domestic assistant. She took two trips to Europe with her stepmother and some young women friends. In England, Addams visited the urban settlement-house program run by Oxford University graduates at Toynbee Hall in London's slums. There she found young men from middle- and upper-class British families living dormitory-style and sharing food, clubs, discussions, and recreational activities with the poorest of London's poor urban dwellers. Toynbee Hall was an inspiration. Jane Addams began to plan for her life work: she, too, would live among the poor in a sincere attempt to establish mutual understanding and cultural exchange.

Though Jane Addams would later be regarded as the pioneer of the American settlement-house movement, she was, in fact, joining an urban reform movement already under way. New York's Neighborhood Guild had been in operation for three years, and the College Settlement Association, organized by a group of Smith College graduates, had opened a settlement in New York in the summer of 1889. By 1891 there would be 6 settlements in the United States, 74 by 1897, and, in 1900, more than 100.

Among the foremost leaders of American settlements were Lillian Wald, who started the Henry Street Settlement in New York City; Mary Kingsbury Simkhovitch, the founder of Greenwich House on New York's Lower East Side; and Mary McDowell, who ran the University of Chicago Settlement House near the Chicago stockyards. Most settlements were run by college graduates, both women and men, and many functioned as short-term residences, where college students could work in a variety of social assistance programs during the summer or for a year or so after graduation.

Once her decision was made, Addams recruited her old college friend Ellen Gates Starr, and spent six months planning, fund raising, and negotiating for public support among influential Chicagoans. Religious leaders and wealthy members of the Chicago Women's Club were particularly eager to help. Among Addams's women supporters were Bertha Honoré Palmer, who would be the president of the Board of Lady Managers for the World's Columbian Exposition of 1893, and Louise deKoven Bowen, who remained a friend of Jane Addams for the rest of her life. "The truth is," Ellen Starr wrote to a friend, "the thing is in the air. People are coming to the conclusion that if anything is to be done about tearing down these walls . . . between classes . . . it must be done by actual contact and done voluntarily from the top. . . . Jane's idea," Starr added, ". . . is that [settlement work] is more for the benefit of the people who do it than for the other class."

On September 18, 1889, not knowing exactly what to expect, but hoping that they would learn from living and giving, Addams and Starr opened the doors of their settlement, Hull House, in a run-down immigrant neighborhood on Chicago's West Side. At first the two women attempted to share art and culture with their neighbors, but very soon they began to respond to more immediate com-

Jane Addams, a founder of the American settlement movement, was idealistic but fundamentally practical and down-to-earth. A great philosopher once told her, "You utter instinctively the truth we others vainly seek."

A singing class at Hull House involves neighborhood residents of all ages. The photographer, Lewis Hine, noted that the music school was "characteristic of the friendly, constructive work that had always been done at Hull House."

munity needs. Within weeks they had a fully operating day nursery, and three years later Hull House had a gymnasium and a playground, an art gallery, a music school for immigrant children, and a little theater in which plays were acted by people from the neighborhood. Hull House residents organized cooking and sewing courses and provided meeting space for some 40 associations and clubs. Eventually, Hull House grew to 13 buildings, including a working women's cooperative house, apartments for married residents and their families, and a coffeehouse/soup kitchen that sold prepared foods cheaply to local working families.

Over the years, many reformers—men as well as women—joined Jane Addams at Hull House, some as residents, some as regular visitors. Distinguished guests included philosophers William James and John Dewey, and President Theodore Roosevelt. For the residents and workers, Hull House provided an exciting intellectual life, a place to discuss social and philosophical issues, and an experimental station where efforts to bridge the gaps between classes were not only talked about, but were put into practice.

It soon became apparent to Jane Addams that clubs and neighborhood services were not enough to counter the poverty and problems of her neighbors. She and a group of Hull House companions pioneered a study of the social conditions in Chicago's 19th Ward, with its tenements, sweatshops, and exploitive child labor. The study was published under the title *Hull-House Maps and Papers* (1895). After this, Hull House residents regularly became involved in political battles for factory inspection and industrial safety, child labor laws, better working conditions for women, the recognition of labor unions, compulsory school attendance, and improved city sanitation.

When Addams herself became incensed with the amount of filth and garbage strewn about the West Side streets, and hundreds of written protests to City Hall brought no improvement in the refuse collection, she secured an appointment as garbage inspector, and, for a while, rose each morning at 6 A.M. to follow the garbagemen around, making sure they did their jobs properly. For many Chicagoans the image of the brave little woman battling the establishment to keep her neighborhood clean was endearing. It cemented Addams's reputation as a practical and determined reformer, just as her willingness to perform the humblest services herself, from baby-sitting to delivering the illegitimate baby of a local teenager, had

This Italian immigrant family occupied a tenement not far from Hull House. Immigrant children often remembered the difficult adjustment to life in American cities. One later wrote: "The sunlight and fresh air of our mountain home were replaced by four walls and people over us . . . the endless monotonous rows of tenement buildings that shut out the sky."

Florence Kelley, who began her career in industrial reform at Hull House, became a galvanic force for social justice. Her friends described her as "explosive, hot-tempered and determined," a "guerilla warrior in the wilderness of industrial wrongs."

persuaded her working-class immigrant neighbors to trust her.

One of Addams's greatest gifts was the ability to attract capable people and put them to work. It would be difficult to imagine a more impressive group of women than those Addams gathered at Hull House in the 1890s and early 1900s. The brilliant and energetic Florence Kelley, educated in Europe, was the divorced mother of three and a socialist. At Hull House, Kelley led an investigation of Chicago sweatshops, and she later was appointed Illinois state factory inspector for child labor. When she moved to New York in the late 1890s, Kelley became secretary of the powerful National Consumers' League, a woman-led reform organization that used the boycott—a refusal to buy certain goods or services—to pressure businesses and industries that exploited workers.

Julia Lathrop took a job with the Illinois Board of Charities and pioneered investigations of the conditions in poorhouses and mental asylums. She and Addams pressured the state legislature into establishing the first U.S. juvenile court, and she was instrumental in founding the Immigrants' Protective League, which provided information, legal services, and employment referral for newcomers to Chicago. In 1912, Lathrop received a Presidential appointment as head of the new U.S. Children's Bureau, a federal agency within the Commerce and Labor Department that had been designed by Florence Kelley and New York settlement leader Lillian Wald.

Alice Hamilton, a doctor from Indiana, became an expert in industrial medicine. Nebraskan Edith Abbott produced a number of classic books on social welfare and became dean of the School of Social Service Administration at the University of Chicago. Her sister, Grace Abbott, headed the U.S. Children's Bureau from 1921 to 1934. Sophonisba Breckinridge, a lawyer from Tennessee, helped Julia Lathrop to found the Chicago Immigrants' Protective League and later became a professor of social economy at the Chicago School of Social Service Administration. Breckinridge was an early and active member of the NAACP and an officer of both the National American Woman Suffrage Association and the American Association of University Women.

The women of Hull House, with the exception of the divorced Florence Kelley, who never remarried, all chose lives as single women. Theirs was an era that still found it difficult to accept the possibility that educated middle-class and elite women might combine marriage and family with a career, although such a pattern was becoming increasingly common for married working-class women. Instead, the Hull House women (and other unmarried settlement workers elsewhere) found richly rewarding lives in the company of like-minded women. They devoted themselves to the causes they cared about, establishing successful careers and earning the respect of political leaders and socially conscious men and women.

In the process of defining their own lives and helping others, these turn-of-the-century career reformers created the profession of social work. Wherever their later lives took them, they never failed to credit the congenial atmosphere of Hull House, where their talents and abilities had matured and responded to the encouragement of Jane Addams. Addams herself, often called "Saint Jane" by the public and the press, was neither saintly nor self-sacrificing, but was, in fact, a woman who took tremendous pleasure in her life and friendships. A consummate organizer, compromiser, fund raiser, and strategist, a compelling writer and speaker, she was the glue that held everything together. Addams became, for many Americans, the symbol of an age of progress and reform.

Increasingly, as women worked through settlement houses and other reform organizations to improve social conditions, they began to confront the reality that they could not accomplish all they wanted to do in public life without being able to vote. Powerless either to endorse or unseat the men in power, they were wearied by endless, and often futile, petition drives and lobbying campaigns to persuade legislators and civic leaders to enact reforms. Between 1890 and 1915, most of the newcomers who joined the fight for woman suffrage would claim that women needed the vote to help clean up America and solve its problems.

The woman suffrage movement, which had amalgamated its two factions in 1890 as the National American Woman Suffrage Association (NAWSA), had gone through a long period of discouragement. As late as 1905, NAWSA's membership still numbered only 17,000. Wyoming Territory had entered the Union as a state in 1890, retaining the full woman suffrage it had had since 1869. Three more states—Colorado, Utah, and Idaho—enfranchised women between 1893 and 1896, giving them the right to vote in all local, state, and

Julia Lathrop, a former resident of Hull House, was concerned with mental health and juvenile justice. In 1912 she became head of the Children's Bureau of the federal government.

national elections. A few states, mostly in the Midwest, allowed women to vote in school or municipal elections, but between 1896 and 1910 nothing but defeat rewarded the petition drives, speaking tours, and lobbying efforts of NAWSA's workers trying to enfranchise women in state-by-state campaigns.

The Western suffrage campaigns of the 1890s and early 1900s were alternately heartening and discouraging. They also taught young NAWSA leaders a number of significant lessons, including the importance of forming individual clubs of suffragists in every voting precinct in the state and the need to win the support of husbands, fathers, and brothers in every community.

The suffrage campaign in South Dakota, waged during the blistering hot summer of 1890, was marked by squabbling between local and national suffrage workers and by the disappearance of promised support from farm and labor organizations. It was a bitter and expensive defeat. Susan B. Anthony, then 70, returned home looking old for the first time in her life, and Carrie Chapman Catt, a young Iowan who would be elected president of NAWSA in 1900 and again in 1915, fell ill with typhoid fever, which nearly killed her.

Catt spent a half year recovering, but she returned to the suffrage movement determined to put the hard lessons of the South Dakota campaign into practice. By 1893, as chairman of NAWSA's business committee, she was able to offer her assistance to the Colorado state suffrage referendum campaign, which had already been under way for some months. Without much assistance from the national organization, a small cadre of dedicated Colorado suffragists had quietly maneuvered a woman suffrage bill through the sleepy state legislature. The bill had been signed by the populist governor, a sympathizer. The women then organized the state referendum campaign in local precincts in 63 Colorado counties, while Catt embarked on a speaking tour in 23 crucial areas. She spoke two or three times in each county, helping to organize 50 new suffrage clubs and enlisting the support of influential men in each key community. She maintained an exhausting pace, traveling by train and horse-drawn wagon in the Rocky Mountains, determined to keep every appointment where voters were waiting for her.

One day Catt missed the train that was to take her down the mountain to her next speaking engagement. The only available ve-

Carrie Chapman Catt in 1901, when she was president of the NAWSA. Catt was a dynamic leader in the fight for woman suffrage. Echoing a battle exhortation from ancient Greece, she once sent a suffragist colleague out on a state campaign with the words:"This is a job. Come through with your shield or upon it."

hicle was a railroad handcar, a small flatbed truck with no engine and minimal brakes and steering. The locals insisted it would take her to her destination in 45 minutes, downhill all the way. Catt climbed aboard but found there was nothing to hold onto except the legs of the driver. Lying as flat as she could, hat and hairpins flying off over the landscape, she steeled her nerves as the handcar careened around the sharp bends, taking the curves on two wheels, threatening to leap off the rails at every turn. A thousand feet below ran a river strewn with boulders. It was called the River of Lost Souls.

At last, disheveled, breathless, and thoroughly shaken, Catt arrived at the bottom of the mountain. She gave her speech on time. Catt's adventures were reported in a suffrage paper, the *Woman's Standard*, and the wild ride became one of her favorite campaign stories. In November 1893 the referendum passed, and Colorado became the second star in the woman suffrage constellation.

A Kansas referendum was defeated in 1894, but woman suffrage passed in Utah and Idaho in the next two years. A hard-fought, carefully conducted California campaign in 1896 looked promising until the final few weeks, when anti-suffrage forces poured a lot of

DON'T FORGET THE WOMEN WHEN YOU VOTE ON TUESDAY.

COLORADO

Equal Rights! Equal Responsibilities! Equal Suffrage!

This cartoon, reminiscent of Abigail Adams's famous warning to her husband, "Remember the ladies," appeared in the Denver Republican *in November 1893. The referendum for woman suffrage passed.*

ANTI SUFFRAGE

SUFFRAGE

THE SANDS OF COMMON SENSE

CHORUS OF ANTIS ["on the glass over, somebody, or it'll be too late!"]

The issue of woman suffrage gave editorial cartoonists plenty of material for their art. This piece showed the progress of the suffrage movement in the 1910s.

money and publicity into a successful last-minute attack on the women's interests. California would not enfranchise its women until 1911.

The anti-suffrage forces were everywhere, though they tended to surface mostly in response to specific woman suffrage campaigns in the states. Especially powerful in the Northeast, anti-suffragists called themselves "remonstrants," though the suffragists liked to call them "antis." Most anti-suffragists believed that woman's subordinate position in society was ordained by God and that woman's weak, gentle nature did not fit her for active participation in the world beyond the home—most especially not for the man's world of politics, with its smoke-filled conventions, rough language, and "shady" transactions. Some argued that if women wanted the vote they would have to bear arms in defense of their country—a possibility few Americans could even contemplate in 1900. Others based their arguments on the widespread 19th-century belief that the basic unit of society was not the individual but the family. The family, they reasoned, needed only one voting member: its male head. Particularly painful to hardworking suffragists was the antis' argument that women did not want suffrage. Indeed, there was plenty of apathy among women, and the number of registered suffragists was undeniably small.

Anti-suffrage sentiment found powerful and influential supporters among conservative clergymen, businessmen, and political and social leaders. Many anti-suffragists were women. Anti-suffragism was also backed by those who made and sold alcoholic beverages, because they tended to associate suffrage with prohibition. The liquor interests feared that if women got the vote they would find a way to ban the sale and consumption of alcohol and their businesses would be ruined. Many suffragists were indeed prohibitionists (many had come to the suffrage movement through the WCTU), but by no means all; and many anti-suffragists were prohibitionists.

For both suffragists and anti-suffragists, race, social class, and ethnic origin were difficult issues. Both sides tended to fear the voting power of recent immigrants (although laws varied from state to state, male immigrants who had applied for citizenship were allowed to vote after a relatively short residence in the United States). Immigrants were often unsophisticated and largely uneducated; their European peasant customs, dress, and speech aroused suspicion and bigotry in middle-class, native-born Americans of both sexes. Anti-suffragists argued that enfranchising women would double the voting power of the "unwashed masses," while suffragists insisted that it was important to let educated women vote so that they could defeat the votes of ignorant foreigners, whom they would outnumber even if immigrant women also received the franchise.

Like the immigrant issue, the subject of votes for African-American women was a complicated one for white suffragists. NAWSA leaders frequently responded negatively to black women's demands for inclusion in suffrage organizations. This practice reflected badly on many otherwise admirable suffrage leaders. Furthermore, as white Southern women began to join the ranks of suffragists in growing numbers around 1900, Northern suffragists found themselves supporting racist arguments in order to win allies for woman suffrage in Southern states. Southern white women activists were certain that the only way to sell woman suffrage to Southern legislators was to convince them that enfranchising white women would guarantee continued white supremacy in the South. Even if black women were to be simultaneously enfranchised, they reasoned, the individual Southern states could find "legal" (and illegal) ways to keep them from voting, similar to those they were already using quite successfully against black men. After the turn of the century, Northern white women suffragists found it expedient to distance themselves from all African-American issues and to allow their white Southern sisters to promote woman suffrage as a tool for white supremacy in their region.

Although some black women suffragists, including Ida B. Wells and Mary Church Terrell, retained more or less cordial relationships with some of the NAWSA leadership and continued to address suffrage conventions, African-American women generally formed their own suffrage organizations. By the early 1900s, there were black women's suffrage clubs and state suffrage organizations all over the country, from Massachusetts to Idaho. Not surprisingly, there was little opposition to woman suffrage among black men, who understood that black women's empowerment would be beneficial to the race as a whole. "Votes for women means votes for Black women," asserted political leader W. E. B. Du Bois.

Between 1896 and 1910, when no new states were enfranchised, NAWSA continued to be a battleground for arguments about race,

THE WEAKER SEX

This cartoon uses an image from classical mythology— Atlas holding the world on his shoulders—to depict the irony of viewing women as the "weaker sex."

At the woman suffrage rally at the capitol building in Richmond, Virginia, a banner maps the progress of woman suffrage around the country. Despite the best efforts of suffragists, the state of Virginia would hold out against women's voting rights throughout the national campaign to pass and ratify the constitutional amendment.

class, and ethnicity. It was also prey to an ongoing internal dispute between those who wished to push for state-by-state enfranchisement of women and those who wanted to work exclusively for a constitutional amendment, which would bring the vote to every woman in the country.

Frustration and discouragement for NAWSA coincided with problems at the highest levels of leadership. Carrie Chapman Catt, who had assumed the NAWSA presidency in 1900, had resigned just four years later to care for her dying husband. Her replacement, Anna Howard Shaw, who held both divinity and medical degrees, was a brilliant and inspiring orator but not a gifted organizer. Susan B. Anthony, who had been for so long a leader, had died in 1906.

It was time for younger suffragists, charged with the enthusiasm of Progressivism, to explore new ideas and tactics in order to inject life into the suffrage movement. Early signs of new life included the creation of two important new organizations in 1901: the Boston

Suffragists took to the streets to dramatize their cause, and parades were a common sight. Anna Howard Shaw (right), who was both a doctor and a minister, served as head of NAWSA from 1904 to 1915.

Equal Suffrage Association for Good Government and the College Equal Suffrage League. Both of these groups grew rapidly and experimented with bold new methods of campaigning: canvassing door to door in city and suburban neighborhoods, staging open-air meetings (suffragists had always previously met, with ladylike decorum, in rented halls or private homes), and touring the state on public transportation to give speeches at every stop. They brought the message to women who might never have gone to a suffrage meeting on their own, and they made many converts.

In 1907, Harriot Stanton Blatch, the daughter of Elizabeth Cady Stanton, started the Equality League of Self-Supporting Women, an alliance of elite women, career women, and working women from factories, laundries, and garment shops in New York. Blatch was convinced that career women and wage-earning women had much in common, and she felt that women should base their demands for political equality on their increasingly important economic role in society.

During her many years of residence in England, Blatch had been impressed by both the British labor movement and the British woman suffrage campaigns. Under her leadership, the Equality League invited English suffragists to speak at their assemblies, where they were enthusiastically received. The league was also the first to send working-class women to address a state legislature on behalf of woman suffrage. By late 1908, the league had a membership of some 19,000.

Like the other new suffrage organizations, the league favored

By 1910, women's labor organizations had become active in the suffrage movement. Within large groups like the Equality League of Self-Supporting Women, founded in 1907, members worked and marched for suffrage alongside business and professional women and social leaders.

open-air meetings, and it was the Equality League that initiated the grand suffrage parades of the 1910s. Parades had a significant impact upon the public consciousness: the spectacle of thousands of working- and middle-class women marching with immense dignity before awed and enthusiastic crowds, and the occasional glimpses of wealthy social leaders among the ranks, were a tremendous boost for the suffragists' cause. Gradually, woman suffrage was becoming "fashionable," and, after more than half a century of struggle, it was now becoming respectable. When the General Federation of Women's Clubs finally endorsed woman suffrage in 1914, it was a sign that the cause had found the mainstream acceptability it had sought for so long.

In 1912, two young suffragists, Alice Paul and Lucy Burns, appeared on the scene, eager to reinvigorate NAWSA with campaign tactics they had learned from frontline participation in the militant wing of the British woman suffrage movement, the so-called suffragettes. Paul and Burns persuaded the NAWSA leadership to let them run NAWSA's Congressional Committee in Washington, D.C., for the purpose of organizing a new drive for a federal constitutional amendment. NAWSA committees around the country would continue to work simultaneously for state-by-state enfranchisement.

The British suffragettes who served as models for Paul and Burns were members of the Women's Social and Political Union, a radical suffrage faction organized by Emmeline Pankhurst and her two daughters, Christabel and Sylvia. The middle-class Pankhursts had both upper- and working-class allies, and they favored the tactics of guerilla warfare in their fight to force the British Parliament to enact woman suffrage. The suffragettes had become adept at disrupting the meetings of male political organizations and regularly provoked their own arrests to gain publicity. Later, they took to breaking windows, pouring acid in mailboxes, and attacking members of Parliament with whips. One suffragette died after she threw herself under the flying hooves of a racehorse owned by King George V. When jailed, the suffragettes were treated not as political prisoners, as they had demanded, but as common criminals. When they went on a hunger strike to protest they were held down and force-fed.

Although Burns and Paul and the other members of the Congressional Committee did not immediately adopt the militant tactics

British suffragette Emmeline Pankhurst, founder of the radical women's Social and Political Union, photographed in Chicago during her first visit to the United States in 1909.

British suffragettes parade in front of Parliament's Big Ben in London, 1910. On November 18 of that year, there was a riot outside the House of Commons at which 120 women were arrested.

The National Woman's Party made Woodrow Wilson and the Democrats, who dominated Congress, the focus of their wrath. They urged those women who could vote to vote against anti-suffrage officials.

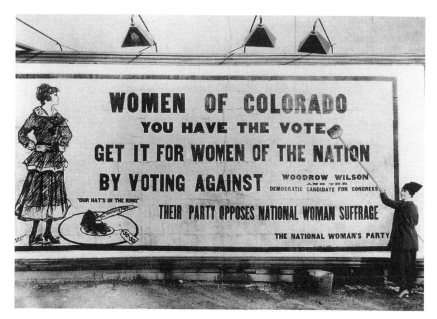

of the British suffragettes, they did make a lot of noise in Washington. They lobbied congressmen unceasingly and, the day before President Woodrow Wilson's inauguration in March 1913, they staged a huge suffrage parade down Pennsylvania Avenue through hostile crowds. The parade culminated in a violent riot when bystanders attacked the suffragists, and the police were forced to call in the cavalry to quell the disturbance.

It soon became apparent that Paul and Burns had a political philosophy antagonistic to that of their more mainstream allies at NAWSA. They believed that the suffrage movement should hold the political party in power responsible for the failure to enact woman suffrage. (In the United States in 1913 that meant the Democrats.) The committee's plan was to embarrass President Wilson, who had not been particularly friendly to woman suffrage, and to work to defeat the Democrats in Congress in the next election.

NAWSA, however, had friends and enemies in all parties and insisted on remaining nonpartisan. On the basis of this irreconcilable issue, and numerous other disagreements, the NAWSA leadership disowned the Congressional Committee, and, in 1914, Burns and Paul set up a separate suffrage organization. Their Congressional Union, which later became the National Woman's Party, remained headquartered in Washington, D.C., where it attracted the most radical elements of the suffrage movement.

Once again the suffrage movement was divided, as it had been between 1868 and 1890, in the days of Lucy Stone and Elizabeth Cady Stanton. However, the passions and concerns that had brought about the split were themselves a sign of increasing vitality in the movement as a whole. In the long run, passage of the federal amendment would be the work of both groups.

In the meantime, NAWSA itself was emerging from years of discouragement. After two cleverly run campaigns based on local appeals featuring billboards, plays, cookbooks, editorials, and church sermons urging voters to "Give the Women a Square Deal," Washington and California had voted for the franchise in 1910 and 1911. These victories were part of a strong Western grass-roots revival that also saw women enfranchised in Kansas, Oregon, and Arizona in 1912. That same year, the Progressive party endorsed woman suffrage during its unsuccessful third-party campaign to elect Theodore Roosevelt, and, in 1913, Illinois enacted a law that allowed its women to vote in Presidential elections. The Illinois suffrage victory, though limited, broke the solid anti-suffrage opposition that had historically prevailed in every state east of the Mississippi River.

In 1915, Carrie Chapman Catt was persuaded to take up the presidency of NAWSA on the retirement of Anna Howard Shaw. Catt had spent the years since her husband's death working to promote the International Woman Suffrage Alliance and, a bit later, managing the New York state suffrage campaign of 1914–15. At this point, no one seriously doubted that women would win the right to vote; it was just a question of time. In 1916, Carrie Catt told a friend she thought it would take six more years.

Woman suffrage headquarters in Cleveland, Ohio, in 1913. Sporting a slogan popularized by President Theodore Roosevelt, its sign demanded that men give women a "square deal" by giving them the right to vote.

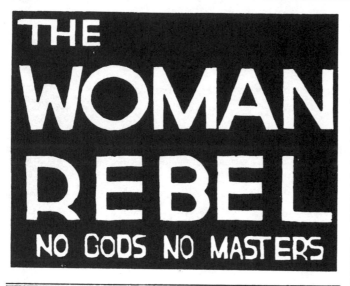

THE WOMAN REBEL

NO GODS NO MASTERS

VOL I.   MARCH 1914   NO. 1.

THE AIM

This paper will not be the champion of any "ism."

All rebel women are invited to contribute to its columns.

The majority of papers usually adjust themselves to the ideas of their readers but the WOMAN REBEL will obstinately refuse to be adjusted.

The aim of this paper will be to stimulate working women to think for themselves and to build up a conscious fighting character.

An early feature will be a series of articles written by the editor for girls from fourteen to eighteen years of age. In this present chaos of sex atmosphere it is difficult for the girl of this uncertain age to know just what to do or really what constitutes clean living without prudishness. All this slushy talk about white slavery, the man painted and described as a hideous vulture pouncing down upon the young, pure and innocent girl, drugging her through the medium of grape juice and lemonade and then dragging her off to his foul den for other men equally as vicious to feed and fatten on her enforced slavery — surely this picture is enough to sicken and disgust every thinking woman and man, who has lived even a few years past the adolescent age. Could any more repulsive and foul conception of sex be given to adolescent girls as a preparation for life than this picture that is being perpetuated by the stupidly ignorant in the name of "sex education"?

If it were possible to get the truth from girls who work in prostitution to-day, I believe most of them would tell you that the first sex experience was with a sweetheart or through the desire for a sweetheart or something impelling within themselves, the nature of which they knew not, neither could they control. Society does not forgive this act when it is based upon the natural impulses and feelings of a young girl. It prefers the other story of the grape juice procurer which makes it easy to shift the blame from its own shoulders, to cast the stone and to evade the unpleasant facts that it alone is responsible for. It sheds sympathetic tears over white slavery, holds the often mythical procurer up as a target, while in reality it is supported by the misery it engenders.

If, as reported, there are approximately 35,000 women working as prostitutes in New York City alone, is it not sane to conclude that some force, some living, powerful, social force is at play to compel these women to work at a trade which involves police persecution, social ostracism and the constant danger of exposure to venereal diseases. From my own knowledge of adolescent girls and from sincere expressions of women working as prostitutes inspired by mutual understanding and confidence I claim that the first sexual act of these so-called wayward girls is partly given, partly desired yet reluctantly so because of the fear of the consequences together with the dread of lost respect of the man. These fears interfere with mutuality of expression —the man becomes conscious of the responsibility of the act and often refuses to see her again, sometimes leaving the town and usually denouncing her as having been with "other fellows." His sole aim is to throw off responsibility. The same uncertainty in these emotions is experienced by girls in marriage in as great a proportion as in the unmarried. After the first experience the life of a girl varies. All these girls do not necessarily go into prostitution. They have had an experience which has not "ruined" them, but rather given them a larger vision of life, stronger feelings and a broader understanding of human nature. The adolescent girl does not understand herself. She is full of contradictions, whims, emotions. For her emotional nature longs for caresses, to touch, to kiss. She is often as well satisfied to hold hands or to go arm in arm with a girl as in the companionship of a boy.

It is these and kindred facts upon which the WOMAN REBEL will dwell from time to time and from which it is hoped the young girl will derive some knowledge of her nature, and conduct her life upon such knowledge.

It will also be the aim of the WOMAN REBEL to advocate the prevention of conception and to impart such knowledge in the columns of this paper.

Other subjects, including the slavery through motherhood; through things, the home, public opinion and so forth, will be dealt with.

It is also the aim of this paper to circulate among those women who work in prostitution; to voice their wrongs; to expose the police persecution which hovers over them and to give free expression to their thoughts, hopes and opinions.

And at all times the WOMAN REBEL will strenuously advocate economic emancipation.

THE NEW FEMINISTS

That apologetic tone of the new American feminists which plainly says "Really, Madam Public Opinion, we are all quite harmless and perfectly respectable" was the keynote of the first and second mass meetings held at Cooper Union on the 17th and 20th of February last.

The ideas advanced were very old and time-worn even to the ordinary church-going woman who reads the magazines and comes in contact with current thought. The "right to work," the "right to ignore fashions," the "right to keep her own name," the "right to organize," the "right of the mother to work"; all these so-called rights fail to arouse enthusiasm because to-day they are all recognized by society and there exist neither laws nor strong opposition to any of them.

It is evident they represent a middle class woman's movement; an echo, but a very weak echo, of the English constitutional suffragists. Consideration of the working woman's freedom was ignored. The problems which affect the

WOMEN IN REBELLION

T hroughout the Progressive Era, the crusade for social reform and women's rights inspired the hard work and dedication of many women. Most reformers were content to work within the existing social and legal systems, but there were others, a handful of rebels, who made it their mission in life to defy society's most basic conventions and to challenge time-honored assumptions about women and women's roles. This small group of writers, artists, philosophers, and radicals proposed sweeping social changes that most turn-of-the-century Americans regarded as threatening and outrageous, if not downright revolutionary.

The radical activities of such women as Charlotte Perkins Gilman, Emma Goldman, Margaret Sanger, and Isadora Duncan—their scandals, their challenges to the law, and their arrests—coincided with the emergence of America's first self-described "feminist" movement, which began its organizational life in the 1910s among a group of freethinkers in New York City's Greenwich Village. These feminists were professionals, writers, journalists, social workers, and labor leaders. A number of them met weekly, calling their group "Heterodoxy" to indicate that only unorthodox opinions would be encouraged. They argued that women's ingrained ideas of appropriate "femininity," their submission, self-sacrifice, and submergence in

The first issue of The Woman Rebel, *published by Margaret Sanger in 1914, was unapologetic in its radical aims and its frank discussion of birth control. Its aim was "to build up a conscious fighting character" in its readers.*

the family were all harmful and outmoded; they demanded full, individual freedom and self-development for all women. Many feminists also sought sexual freedom outside of marriage, risking social condemnation by daring to flout convention and respectability with their love affairs.

Early 20th-century feminism had roots in socialism and links to the suffrage movement, though not all suffragists were feminists by any means. Although feminist demands for personal freedom, meaningful work, and free sexual expression shocked many, feminism gave heart to others. After 1920, it became the vanguard of the 20th-century women's movement.

When Charlotte Perkins Gilman joined Heterodoxy in 1912 she was already one of the most important social theorists of her era. Born in 1860, she was the grandniece of Catharine Beecher and Harriet Beecher Stowe, and very proud to be a Beecher—though she turned out to be a far more original thinker than either of her eminent aunts. Her childhood was clouded by her father's desertion and the family's consequent descent into genteel poverty. Charlotte's education was erratic and limited, and after attending the Rhode Island School of Design, she supported herself by teaching art and designing greeting cards until she married Charles Walter Stetson in 1884.

A daughter, Katharine, was born a year later, and Charlotte, not temperamentally equipped to cope with the demands of mother-

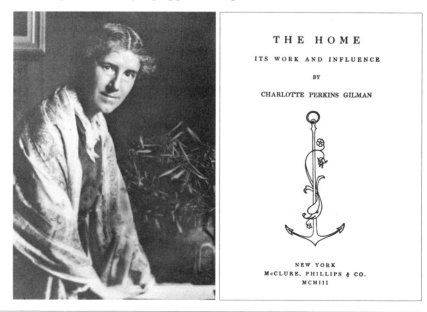

In The Home *(1903), Charlotte Perkins Gilman questioned accepted truths about American home life and proposed a number of domestic innovations. She also advocated outside jobs and economic independence for women.*

THE HOME

ITS WORK AND INFLUENCE

BY

CHARLOTTE PERKINS GILMAN

NEW YORK
McCLURE, PHILLIPS & CO.
MCMIII

hood, soon suffered a nervous breakdown. She was sent to see an expert on nervous conditions, who prescribed bed rest and isolation. The doctor ordered her never to paint or write again, but to devote herself solely to the care of her husband and baby. To Charlotte, who had been painting and writing since before her marriage and who loved swimming and gymnastics, the prescription was like a death sentence. She grew worse instead of better. Within a matter of months, however, Charlotte found the courage to disobey the doctor's orders. She separated from her husband and, taking little Katharine, went to live in California. There she became attracted to the work and ideas of suffragists and labor leaders and to a popular new form of socialism. This new American version promoted a global, cooperative society to be achieved through gradual, peaceful change, not through class struggle and violence. Charlotte began to write and then to lecture, becoming well known as a speaker on economic and social topics. She was soon totally self-supporting and grew stronger and saner with each passing week.

In 1892, the year in which she published her most famous short story, "The Yellow Wallpaper," a fictional account of her breakdown, Charlotte divorced her husband. Not long afterward, she sent her daughter to live with him and his new wife. The choice to surrender custody of her child created a scandal that swirled around Charlotte's head for several years: not only had she rejected an apparently amiable husband, but she had abandoned her child and repudiated the cherished American domestic ideal. It was nearly 10 years later that Charlotte took another chance on marriage. This time she chose her first cousin, George Houghton Gilman, seven years her junior and a lifelong friend. This marriage was a success, bringing companionship and full support for her work.

Charlotte Perkins Gilman's books and short stories, and her magazine, *The Forerunner,* reflect her own struggles as a woman and her perceptions of women's role in history and society. In *Women and Economics* (1898), her most important book, she concluded that women's historical dependence on men for sustenance had warped their potential to be fully human, because sexual and reproductive characteristics calculated to attract men had evolved at the expense of women's intellectual and spiritual qualities. Men, in turn, had been cheated of life's fullness by their need to dominate women and

Starting a Community Kitchen

Just How it Can be Done With Little Outlay

By Myrtle Perrigo Fox and Ethel Lendrum, Home Demonstration Agent

HERE is a chance for a woman gifted with common sense, some business ability, and a fair knowledge of cookery, not only to rescue or relieve other women, but to add to the family income or even to earn her livelihood. You can start a community kitchen with three or four families as patrons. Serve two meals a week until you are asked to cook more. A modest beginning will enable you to gain your capital and experience at the same time.

Do not force your meals upon anyone. Make none of your patrons feel that it is their duty to buy from you. Let them all understand clearly that they need patronize you only when it serves their own interests to do so.

You need no extra equipment to begin with and no capital. You can start in your own kitchen with the utensils you use for your own meals.

We started a kitchen because we wanted it established ourselves, and it is popular because our neighbors' needs coincide with ours. We have served twenty two people at a time—no more only because we were not ready to cook for them.

People who are accustomed to maids, but have been unable to find them, people who cannot afford them, people who do not like to have them about, families with invalid mothers, women who earn their own living—all are glad to buy these ready-to-serve meals.

We have started a kitchen in a public school located in a neighborhood where the mothers do not know how to feed their families, and they marvel at the results we produce for twenty-five cents. As a matter of fact, when the school girls do the cooking we can furnish a meal for less. They are planning soon to feed one hundred from their kitchen.

It means real economy in the purchase of food, not only because we buy in quantities, but because we buy only what is needed to provide well-balanced meals.

It means better-cooked meals. One skilled cook gives her undivided attention to the work, instead of having it done by many bad cooks.

It means a saving of fuel.

And it means a saving of talent. Many a gifted woman has been spoiled to make a poor housekeeper.

The meals served from a community kitchen will not be beyond the average purse. On a cash-and-carry basis you can serve a good dinner for twenty-five cents. You can add a delivery charge of ten cents if your patrons prefer service. Schoolboys gladly earn the dimes.

THE problem of cooking these meals in one place is simple, but there are many pitfalls between the kitchen and the dinner table. You cannot walk the streets with a platter of meat in one hand and a bowl of soup in the other. They would not stay hot if you could.

When we were considering the question of containers we looked about for something easy to handle, easy to obtain, easy to replace. Fruit jars slipped into cases made from cylindrical cereal cartons answered the question. A one and a half pound oatmeal carton can be rolled in newspaper cut to fit and slipped into the larger three-pound carton. Asbestos pipe covering may be used for the inner lining, but it costs more.

To serve a family of four, you need three cases, one quart jar, two pint jars, one half-pint bottle, one baking-powder or cocoa tin and perhaps a bowl or a pan for a meat loaf. These containers will easily fit into an ordinary market basket.

To make the cases, use two three-pound oatmeal or coffee cartons, two smaller oatmeal cartons, which will hold quart jars, and two cartons just large enough for pint jars. Have your patrons own their baskets and containers, and tell them that when they want dinners they must bring their baskets beforehand. Nothing spoils a good dinner more quickly than having no containers to serve it in.

TO MAKE your meal satisfactory to your patrons your food combinations must be carefully chosen. To make your venture profitable to yourself your food costs must be carefully considered. To be served, the food must fit into your containers.

If you are serving twenty people with dinners at twenty-five cents each you must not spend more than three dollars and fifty cents for food. If you buy it for less your profit will be so

The Cooked Dinner on the "Cash-and-Carry" Plan

quantities of the various foods you will buy. So there are four stages in your meal plan:

1. Decide upon your menu.
2. Look it over to see whether it will go into the containers.
3. Determine your quantities.
4. Figure up the costs to see if you can afford to serve the meal.

POTATOES can be served escalloped, creamed, au gratin, mashed or baked, or they can go into a stew.

Roasts, fillet of beef, pork tenderloin frenched, meat loaf and stew are easily packed.

Serve the vegetables and salads that are in season in your own locality. In spring and midsummer vegetable salads are perhaps most appetizing, or strawberries and pineapples can be used. In winter, apples, grapefruit, oranges and bananas furnish good foundations. Coleslaw is in season a large part of the year.

For desserts you can use frosted cup cakes or cookies, steamed pudding with sauce, fruit custard and strawberry shortcake.

There is this to remember: The bigger the variety the smaller portions of each item you need serve. You can thus make the whole cost of the meal less by adding inexpensive items like soup or vegetables and serving smaller portions of your expensive meats or fruit salads. Your meal will not only be cheaper, but it will be more satisfying. You will please both your patrons and yourself. While the so-called one-dish meals will do for suppers or lunches, they do not make satisfactory dinners, partly because they do not look like enough when served.

The Community Kitchen Dinner Served at Home

MEATS and potatoes, vegetables, soups, salads and some desserts can be packed in quart and pint jars. Your meats you can slice and slip into a jar on top of potatoes. Fillet of beef, pork tenderloin frenched, even meat loaf, can be served in the same way. Or, if you wish to, you can bake and serve your meat loaf in agate bowls or in small bread tins.

If you don't need them for steamed pudding your meat can be served in your baking-powder tins. Stew can be served in quart jars. Swiss steak can be put into a pint jar with gravy over it. Cakes and cookies can be wrapped in oil paper.

By taking the inner carton out of a large container you can pack baked potatoes, steamed puddings in their baking powder tins and perhaps pint or half pint jars of gravy or dressing together. In summer it would be well to put the cold things in cartons to keep them chilled.

When you have bought your food, the next thing you do is to make sure you have a basket for every family to be served, plainly marked with the name and number of portions desired and the proper number and kinds of containers.

will enable you to pack your food at least an hour ahead of mealtime.

Make your desserts first, unless the meat calls for long-time cooking. When you have put your meat and vegetables on the fire, and your jars for the hot foods are warming in the oven or on the back of the stove, you can pack your salads and desserts. Place salads and cold desserts in the ice box in summer, or outdoors in cold weather, and hot desserts in the oven.

Pack your hot foods, meat, vegetables, soups, and so forth, and put them into the oven. The funnel you used in your canning will come in handy. When thoroughly heated, slip jars into the cases, stuffing crumpled paper into any crevices which may be left. Put covers tightly on the cartons and place them in the proper baskets. Before you part with your baskets, check them all up carefully to make sure each patron has all the kinds and the proper quantities of food. Your mind will rest much easier if you can say to yourself: "I know I put meat in every basket."

NOW, let us suppose you have received orders for twenty dinners, not families. Try for your menu the following:

Pork Tenderloin With Gravy
Mashed Potatoes
Buttered Carrots
Strawberry Shortcake

Twenty pieces of pork tenderloin frenched will weigh about two pounds and a quarter. One peck of potatoes will be sufficient. The number of carrots will depend entirely upon their size. Four quarts of berries will do, although of course "the berrier the better." Double the shortcake receipt which calls for two cupfuls of flour. Now see if you can afford to buy this meal:

2¼ pounds of pork tenderloin, at 45 cents	$1.02
1 Peck of potatoes	.35
Carrots	.20
¼ Pound of butter	.15
1 Quart of milk	.13
Fat for meat and gravy	.05
1 Pound of flour	.07
2 Ounces of fat, at 20 cents a pound	.03
Baking powder and salt	.01
Strawberries, at 15 cents a quart	.60
Sugar, at 10 cents a pound	.10
	$2.71

You see you are well under your three-dollar-and-fifty-cent limit; and if you feel that your patrons will not be satisfied with this meal you can increase the quantity of meat or add another vegetable or a salad.

Now, let us pack up this meal for a family of four. The meat and potatoes will go into the quart jar. A pint jar will do for the carrots, another for the strawberries, the half-pint bottle for the gravy. The potatoes will go into the quart case; the carrots into the pint case; take the inner carton out of the other large case and put in the bottle of gravy, with the paper-wrapped biscuits on top. The jar of strawberries can be slipped into the extra inner carton.

SUPPOSE you take another menu. Try the following this time:

Asparagus Soup
Meat Loaf With Escalloped Potatoes
Pineapple-and-Strawberry Salad
Chocolate Cup Cakes

This calls for one large bunch of asparagus, five pounds of chopped meat, one loaf of bread and one egg, a little seasoning, three pineapples, one quart of strawberries and three heads of lettuce.

A recipe using a cupful and a half of flour will make the cup cakes, with the addition of one square of chocolate and one cupful of sugar for the frosting.

The soup will take a pint jar, the potatoes a quart jar and the gravy a half-pint bottle; the salad, a pint, and the meat loaf can be put into the baking-powder tin, the chocolate cup cakes wrapped in paper.

This meal will cost:

1 Bunch of asparagus	$ .15
2 Quarts of milk	.26
4 Pounds of beef, at 25 cents a pound	1.00
¾ Peck of potatoes, at 35 cents a peck	.24
1 Quart of strawberries	.15
3 Pineapples, at 15 cents each	.45
3 Heads of lettuce	.15
Cup cakes	.23
Bread for the loaf	.08
1 Egg	.04
Seasonings	.05
	$2.80

The June 1919 issue of the Ladies' Home Journal *included this forward-looking advice on setting up a community kitchen. The facility operated by the writers served 22 people, who were required to provide their own containers to transport food. Neighborhood children were paid to make deliveries.*

deny their humanity.

As a solution to fundamental inequities, Gilman proposed in her later writings a communally organized society that would liberate women from full-time domestic service to men. The private home and monogamous (single-spouse) marriages would continue to exist, but women would be freed from cooking, cleaning, laundry, and child care by the reorganization of those jobs within the community. Women would be able to develop their fullest capacities and find meaningful work and economic independence. The home would be a place of rest and congeniality rather than a workplace, and women, now fully equal to men, would be far better mothers and happier wives.

Born in 1869, nine years later than Charlotte Perkins Gilman and half a world away, Emma Goldman, the daughter of a Jewish shopkeeper, spent her childhood in the repressive atmosphere of czarist Russia. As a teenager in St. Petersburg she read radical literature and befriended revolutionary students. In 1885 she emigrated to the United States, where she found work in a factory in Rochester, New York, and, after a brief, unhappy marriage and divorce, settled in New York City. Her combative spirit was fired by social injustice and by the huge gulf that she saw between the American dream and the American reality for those on the bottom of society. Goldman loved America, but she wanted to improve it. Before long, she had become involved with Johann Most and Alexander Berkman, leaders of the American wing of the international anarchist movement. (Anarchism envisioned a world organized into small, cooperative industries, farms, and villages, which operated without any coercive laws or government intervention. Everyone would be equal, and no person would grow rich from another person's labor. If necessary, anarchists argued, this ideal world would have to be brought about by the destruction of the existing order through revolution and individual acts of violence.)

In 1892, Goldman offered her support to Alexander Berkman when he attempted to assassinate industrialist Henry Clay Frick. When the attack failed, Berkman went to jail for 14 years and Goldman, who had not actually participated, fell under the intense scrutiny of police and federal authorities. This surveillance would dog her for the rest of her life in America. She was arrested and jailed on many

Anarchist Emma Goldman ("Red Emma") was a lifelong advocate of free speech and women's rights. One journalist called her "the daughter of the dream," whose "vision is the vision of every great-souled man or woman who has ever lived."

Standing up in the back of a car, Emma Goldman addresses an open-air rally in New York's Union Square in 1916.

occasions. In 1901 authorities even tried—unsuccessfully—to link Goldman to the assassination of President William McKinley, though she had long since abandoned her belief in violence as a tool for social change.

Through much of her career, Goldman focused her considerable talents on social ills and women's emancipation. She published a radical magazine, *Mother Earth,* and crisscrossed the country delivering lectures on labor and anarchism, on birth control (which she felt would free women from their historical bondage to reproduction), and on marriage (which she labeled legalized prostitution, a parasitic relationship based on the treatment of women as property). Goldman favored free love—not promiscuity, as her critics feared, but a free association of equally independent men and women. She herself had many lovers in her lifetime, and a host of loyal friends.

In general, Goldman was impatient with Progressive Era politics and women's reform organizations. Suffrage, she felt, was a distraction from the real need to change society at its roots. She had her doubts about settlement work, too, asking what use it was to teach the poor how to eat with a fork "if they have not the food." Goldman was one of the most charismatic and magnetic speakers America had ever seen and an avid champion of free speech. In one town, threatened with arrest if she appeared on the speakers' platform, she walked in with her hands raised and a handkerchief stuffed in her mouth. The crowd was ecstatic, and Goldman made her point without uttering a single word.

Nearly everyone had an opinion about Emma Goldman. To some, like journalist William Marion Reedy, she was one of the world's greatest living women, an enlightened soul born "eight thousand years ahead of her age." To others she was the most dangerous "Red" in America. Both evaluations were true. Goldman was dangerous, not because she embraced anarchism, but because she presented a real challenge to people's ideas about the fundamental values of American culture: about gender relations, materialism, the class structure, and the role of government in free society.

In 1917, Goldman and her old friend Alexander Berkman were arrested and imprisoned for their active opposition to the military draft for World War I. When they were released two years later, in the middle of the United States's postwar "Red Scare," the government deprived them of citizenship and deported them to Russia, along with a number of other radicals. Goldman spent the rest of her life in exile in Europe.

Margaret Sanger (1878–1966) owed a significant debt to Emma Goldman, who was promoting birth control in the United States before Sanger adopted the cause and made it her life work. But Sanger, though she had been a socialist in the 1910s, was not a revolutionary, and she succeeded where the defiantly radical Goldman could not, eventually making the birth control reform movement acceptable to large numbers of Americans.

As a young woman, Sanger witnessed the premature death of her own mother, who had been worn out by multiple childbirths and the strain of raising 11 children on her husband's artisan wages. A few years later, married and working as a nurse in New York City's immigrant slums, Sanger saw firsthand the unhealthy children and squalid,

Margaret Sanger used this 1916 publicity photo, taken with sons Stuart and Grant, when she returned from Europe to face charges of misuse of the mails to send birth control literature.

foreshortened lives of women whose families were too large; she witnessed the pain in which many died from clumsy, back-room abortions. Ignorant herself about effective methods of birth control and powerless to help her patients, Sanger seethed with frustration. In 1913, seeking some answers in Europe, she found government-sponsored birth control clinics, staffed by doctors and nurses, where married women could receive information about limiting the size of their families and be fitted with devices to prevent conception.

Sanger was frustrated in all her early attempts to make birth control systematically available to American women. Written infor-

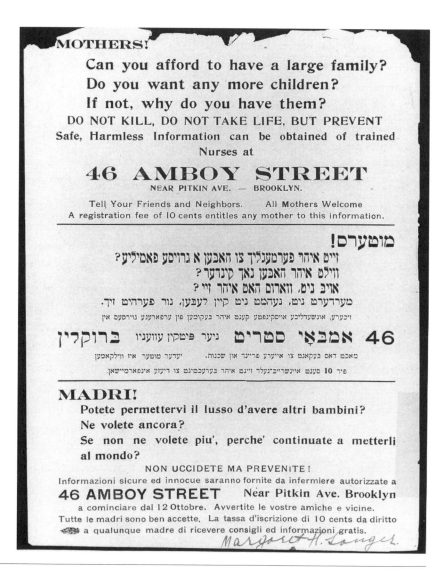

This circular, printed in English, Yiddish, and Italian, advertised Sanger's clinic in the Brownsville section of Brooklyn, New York. This was the first birth control clinic in the country.

mation about contraception was considered obscene and classed with pornography; it was illegal for anyone to tell another person anything about contraception or provide contraceptive materials. Historically conservative, not to say prudish, Americans were reluctant to discuss sexuality or its consequences, and many feared that the limitation of family size among the white middle classes would amount to a form of "race suicide," in which the "best" people would rapidly be outnumbered by the offspring of poor, immigrant, or black Americans.

But Margaret Sanger was interested in birth control for all women, especially the poor, who had so few choices in their lives. In 1914, she was arrested and her birth control publications banned from distribution under the obscenity regulations of the U.S. Post Office Department. Given insufficient time to prepare her legal defense, Sanger avoided a jail sentence by fleeing to Europe for a few months, though it meant leaving her three young children behind.

In 1916, Sanger and her sister, Ethel Byrne, a nurse, were arrested for opening an experimental birth control clinic in the slums of Brooklyn, New York. The clinic was closed down, to the despair of its women clients, and Sanger and her sister went to jail.

Public support and sympathy for Sanger's crusade grew rapidly

Sanger appears in court to defend her actions on behalf of birth control.

after 1916, involving the efforts of both college-educated and working-class women. By the 1920s, there were national and international birth control leagues, and little by little the U.S. legal system gave way before insistent demands for reproductive control from women's organizations and from physicians. Margaret Sanger remained active in the promotion of birth control and the pioneering of new contraceptive methods until her death in 1966.

Isadora Duncan (1878–1927) was born to break the rules. Raised in San Francisco after her parents' divorce, she and her sister and brothers were brought up by their antimaterialistic and atheistic mother, who instilled in them a love of poetry, dance, music, and nature. As a very young girl, Duncan decided it would be her mission to rescue the art of dance from what she saw as the unnatural rigidity of classical 19th-century ballet. She hoped to restore the expressive qualities dance had lost since the time of the ancient Greeks. Duncan studied sculpture and nature and the organic movements of the human body, always seeking ways to make dance express the meaning of music, great ideas, or profound and primitive human emotions. She was convinced that all energy and movement originated in the solar plexus (in the center of the abdomen), rather than the spine, which was the center of all balletic dance movements; toe dancing she dismissed as ugly and artificial. Her use of prone or supine positions, bent backs and knees, her abandonment of frothy tutus in favor of tunics, flowing draperies, and bare feet, have all become part of modern dance as we know it today.

Duncan never found support among American audiences. Turn-of-the-century Americans were not comfortable with her unorthodox style of movement or with her diaphanous draperies, which were deliberately designed to reveal the body as it moved. Briefly, at the beginning of her career, Duncan attracted the attention of a few rich New York socialites, who hired her to dance as salon entertainment; a few years later, Americans would be too shocked by her numerous, highly publicized love affairs and by the births of her illegitimate children to want to pay to see her in her own country. Europeans were far more welcoming; they found Duncan colorful and daring and seemed to appreciate her art.

After 1900, Duncan lived most of the rest of her life in Europe, where she toured with her performances and ran dance schools for gifted young girls. Duncan was frequently acclaimed, and European artists, from musicians to painters, saw her as the embodiment of the future of art. The French sculptor Auguste Rodin said that he sometimes felt Duncan was the greatest woman the world had ever known.

The triumphs of Duncan's life were counterweighted with trag-

The daring dancer Isadora Duncan favored flowing tunics and expressive, free movements. A critic in the Russian city of St. Petersburg wrote, "There is so much sculpture in her, so much color and simplicity, that she fully deserves the capacity audiences."

edy. In 1913, in France, her two little children were drowned when a car they were sitting in slipped its brakes and rolled into the River Seine. Duncan never recovered from their deaths and was haunted until the end of her life by her last vision of their faces in the car window as the chauffeur drove them away. Her own death at age 49 came in 1927, just a few weeks after she had completed her autobiography, *My Life*. Climbing into an open sports car in the French Riviera town of Nice, she called out to some friends seated in a sidewalk café: "Adieu mes amis. Je vais à la gloire!" ("Good-bye my friends. I am going to glory!") A moment later, as the car pulled away, her long, fringed scarf caught in the spokes of a rear wheel and broke her neck. She died instantly.

It would be decades before the achievements of Isadora Duncan and other cultural radicals were fully appreciated in America. However, their courageous rejection of conventions in both art and life

Duncan found relatively little acceptance in the United States and for many years lived in France. The fringed red shawl she wears in this 1920 photo later killed her in a freak automobile accident.

was already beginning to find echoes in the larger society in the years just before World War I. Symbolized by new fashions in women's clothing and by changes in manners and behavior, women's tentative rebellion against the rigid morality of the 19th century had begun. And it was taking place not just among a small cadre of urban feminists, but among well-brought-up young ladies all across the country. Respectable women everywhere abandoned their corsets and began to wear skirts that exposed their ankles; all over the country young ladies joined the dance craze, hopping, stepping, and gliding to the Bunny Hug and the Turkey Trot, often in close proximity to their partners. Gradually, ordinary middle- and working-class women were altering the social definition of sexual morality and stretching the boundaries of female respectability. These cultural changes would shortly find even more dramatic expression in the era known as the Roaring Twenties.

CHAPTER 7

WOMEN IN
WAR AND PEACE

I n 1914, across the Atlantic Ocean from the United States, a
small conflict in the Balkan countries escalated into a continental war involving most of Europe. The war pitted the
nations of the Central Powers—Germany, Austria-Hungary,
and the Ottoman Empire (Turkey)—against the Allies—England,
France, Belgium, Russia, Serbia, and Montenegro. Before long, the
effects of the European conflict began to touch the lives of distant
Americans, impinging upon the national sense of safety and forcing
conscientious men and women to choose between militarism and
pacifism. The war altered the work and family lives of women of all
social classes; it also challenged the strategies of both factions of the
woman suffrage movement, even as it provided the stage for the
final campaign.

President Woodrow Wilson had found it impossible to sustain
American neutrality after German submarines began to attack American
shipping in 1915. In April 1917, he asked Congress to declare war
on Germany. Among the few dissenting votes in a chorus of support
for this popular war was that of Jeannette Rankin, a representative
from Montana and the only woman in Congress.

U.S. involvement in World War I lasted only 19 months, but
some 4 million American men were drafted during the course of the

*Goverment posters advertised
the need for women to apply
their domestic skills, such as
gardening and canning, to the
war effort. The artist for this
poster was the noted James
Montgomery Flagg.*

American women staff an American Red Cross canteen in Paris where refugee families were given clothing, food, and other assistance.

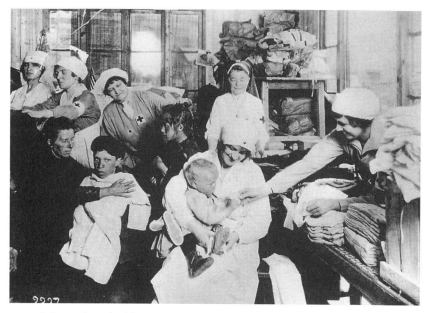

war. More than half were sent overseas to the battlefields of France. Enlisted to serve in the armed forces as support staff and nurses were the women of the Army Nurse Corps and some 11,000 Navy "yeomanettes." There were also 305 Marine Corps "marinettes." Professional nurses for the army were recruited through the Red Cross, which enrolled more than 20,000 of them. The Red Cross also recruited a large number of aides, clerks, and social workers to assist with the war effort at home and abroad.

Molly Dewson and Polly Porter, two social workers from Massachusetts, served with the Red Cross in France for 15 months, engaged in the task of resettling French and Belgian refugees who had fled their homes in the war-ravaged areas of the battlefront. Dewson and Porter were stationed so far behind the front lines that they never even heard gunfire, yet they were glad they had been given a chance to be useful.

American women who did not go abroad were encouraged to serve their country in a variety of voluntary ways. Many started victory gardens to grow their own food, and many canned what they had grown to help save commercial supplies for the troops. Housewives invented ways to serve meatless, wheatless, or butterless meals. Some women started wearing shorter skirts in order to save cloth. Women's clubs and church and civic groups organized war bond drives to help raise funds for the war effort; they rolled bandages and prepared supplies for the Red Cross; and they worked for government war relief agencies. As in all wars, women took over the management of farms and small businesses that their husbands left behind when they enlisted.

Not all American women supported their country's participation in the war. As early as 1915, in response to escalating violence in Europe and widespread apprehension that the United States would soon be directly involved, a number of prominent women activists had created the Woman's Peace Party (WPP). The 3,000 original members of the WPP—among them such notable figures as Jane Addams, Carrie Chapman Catt, and Charlotte Perkins Gilman—adopted a peace platform that called for arms limitation for all nations and for immediate and ongoing mediation of the European conflict. They linked their demand for a voice in the decision making with a protest of the atrocities of war: "As women we are particularly charged with the future of childhood and with the care of the helpless and the unfortunate. We will no longer endure without protest that added burden of maimed and invalid men and poverty-stricken widows and orphans which was placed upon us [in past wars]. . . . We demand that women be given a share in deciding between war and peace."

In April 1915, American delegates from the WPP traveled to an International Congress of Women in the Netherlands. Women from

The United States delegation to the International Congress of Women at the Hague, 1915. Many of these women were members of the American Women's Peace Party, a group dedicated to ending the war in Europe.

Jane Addams (right) with colleague Mary McDowell of the University of Chicago Settlement. Many community workers also took up the cause of peace. Addams was awarded the Nobel Peace Prize in 1931.

both the Central Powers and the Allied nations attended the conference. Chairman Jane Addams, who represented the largest neutral nation, told a reporter, "The great achievement of this congress is . . . the getting together of these women from all parts of Europe when their men folks are shooting each other from opposite trenches."

A number of American women withdrew from the peace movement when their country joined the Allied forces in 1917. Sadly, but wholeheartedly, they offered their assistance in what President Wilson called a war to "make the world safe for democracy." Those who remained pacifists were reviled in the press and greeted with jeers when they spoke in public. Hysterical patriots waged a campaign of suspicion and resentment against Jane Addams and others whom they considered "reds" or even German sympathizers. "Saint Jane," the woman who had represented nobility and unselfishness to a whole generation of Americans, was branded a coward and a traitor. More than a decade would pass before Addams's reputation was restored and her pacifism understood. In 1931, she received the Nobel Peace Prize.

For American working women, World War I brought an unprecedented boon in employment opportunities. As men enlisted in the armed forces or were drafted, they left behind jobs in industry and business that had never previously been open to women. The departure of the regular workers, combined with the enormous Allied demand for munitions and war support materials, helped to produce a labor vacuum that women rushed to fill. Tens of thousands of new jobs opened up. Iron and steel mills, munitions factories, chemical and electrical industries all sought women workers.

Women happily shifted from traditional women's jobs in domestic service and unskilled factory labor to the more demanding and better paying wartime jobs. A number of women were joining the paid labor force for the first time, but most of the growth in women's work took place among those who were already working for wages. At one point during the war, women comprised 20 percent or more of all workers manufacturing airplanes, electrical machinery, leather and rubber goods, food, and printed materials. Women in industry ran presses and drills, lathes, welding tools, and milling machines; a few even operated cranes.

Labor unions, which enrolled nearly 3 million new members during the war, increasingly included women members. The U.S. Department of Labor opened a subdivision called the Woman in Industry Service to oversee working conditions and hours of labor for women. The service later became the Women's Bureau of the Department of Labor.

The U.S. government recruited thousands of young typists and stenographers for wartime clerical service in Washington, D.C. Another attractive opportunity for women came from the railroads, which had been placed under government control in late 1917. Women railroad employees worked as station clerks and dispatchers, car cleaners, and as rail yard laborers. By the end of the war, more than 100,000 women were employed in railroad work, where they were given good wages, an eight-hour day, and opportunities for promotion. Even in the relatively enlightened railroad industry, however, women still encountered job segregation and sexual harrassment, and craftsmen still maintained exclusive access to many skilled jobs, just as they had in the prewar workplace.

In their home communities, women took jobs as conductors, ticket takers, and station agents in public transportation. Conducting was particularly attractive because its hours could be structured around family needs and it paid more than twice as much as most women's work—an average of $21 a week instead of $8 to $10. In general, wages for women war workers were higher than anything that they had previously experienced, often two or three times what they earned in traditional women's jobs—though unless the indus-

Women workers, such as this factory worker, encountered stiff opposition from their male colleagues, and some unions excluded them in the hope that they would leave the factories at the end of the war.

Women streetcar conductors in New York City, 1917. During the war, 12 American cities employed several hundred women in such jobs. The conductors' unions protested vigorously, and one used the slogan "Keep the Girls Off the Cars."

try was unionized or under government control, wages were not necessarily as high as those of men in the same jobs.

For many African Americans, the war brought geographical changes as well as changes in employment. During the Great Migration of 1915 to 1920, some 500,000 Southern black men and women left for Northern cities, where industrial labor shortages caused by the call-up of white men had created unheard-of opportunities. As white women replaced white men in industry and business, black women were able to move into the jobs that the white women had vacated. The wages were especially attractive: a cook or a laundress could earn in a day what she earned in a week in the South; in industry she could earn $3 a day, compared to 50 cents for picking cotton. Domestic service paid twice what it did in the South. Railroads hired black women as cleaners and yard workers and paid government-regulated wages. Despite these advantages, the persistence of racism in the North meant that many black women were paid 10 to 60 percent less than white women doing similar work and that they were always assigned to the hottest, dirtiest, and most disagreeable tasks available. Although African-American women increased their participation in Northern industry by 100 percent, they remained less than 7 percent of the women's industrial labor force.

When the armistice was signed on November 11, 1918, and soldiers returned home, it was not surprising that women everywhere were reluctant to give up their wartime jobs. Those who had joined unions specifically to protect their jobs often found that male union

As white women moved into men's jobs in skilled trades, black women also took untraditional work, but in lower-level and more physically strenuous jobs. Here, black women load wheelbarrows in a brickyard.

leaders were as anxious as the rest of society to see women return to domestic life. For most women, losing a wartime job meant a return, not to domestic chores—which they would be performing in any case—but to low-paid, sex-segregated women's work. In the end, women were unable to hold on to most skilled jobs in heavy industry, in steel, or in railroad work, though they did manage to preserve gains that they had made in the food and garment industries.

Telephone operators and office workers, whose job market had been expanding even before the war, continued to make gains. Black women at every level of the labor force dropped a few notches, and those at the bottom were pushed out altogether. Some went home to the South, but many more stayed in Northern cities, piecing together lives that included both work and family. They reproduced in their city neighborhoods the same sort of supportive networks of kin and friends that had helped to sustain them in the South.

The last campaign in the fight for woman suffrage took place amid the tensions and excitement of war and the immediate postwar years. In 1915, state suffrage referenda in New York, New Jersey, Massachusetts, and Pennsylvania had been defeated, which meant that the supporters of woman suffrage still did not have a single urbanized, industrialized Eastern state in their camp. Undeterred, suffragists regrouped, raised more money, and plunged back into the fight. Under the new NAWSA leadership, with Carrie Chapman Catt as president and Maud Wood Park in charge of the congressional lobbying operation in Washington, D.C., NAWSA adopted the "Winning Plan": they would continue to work for suffrage in the individual states because they needed the expanded electorate that newly enfranchised states would bring, and they would also increase the pressure on the U.S. Congress to pass the constitutional amendment. Park and her fellow lobbyists maintained extensive files on each congressman and senator and carefully selected individual women to talk with them in an attempt to win them over.

In the course of the 1916 election campaign both the Republican and Democratic parties had endorsed woman suffrage but left the decision up to the individual states. Once safely reelected, Wilson let the subject of woman suffrage drop. During his first address to Congress after the election, Wilson pretended to ignore a large banner unfurled from the gallery by Alice Paul and members of the

This cartoon originally ran in the New York World *and was then reprinted in papers around the country. It shows anti-suffragists celebrating defeat of woman suffrage in New Jersey in 1915. Suffrage was also defeated in New York and Pennsylvania that same year.*

"WELL, BOYS, WE SAVED THE HOME."

National Woman's Party, the radical faction of the suffrage movement. The banner read, "Mr. President, What Will You Do for Woman Suffrage?" A few weeks later, in early 1917, the National Woman's Party began systematically to picket the White House, and on Wilson's inaugural day a thousand women marched solemnly around and around outside the heavy iron fence.

No one, including the President, would be able to ignore woman suffrage much longer. The campaign was receiving front page coverage in newspapers all over the country; it was featured prominently in popular magazines; the national environment was growing daily more supportive; and 4 million women in 11 states could now vote. If they could add one large Eastern state, women would have enough political power to push toward the amendment and to unseat congressmen and senators who refused to convert to the cause.

During World War I members of the National Woman's Party picketed the White House for six months to badger the President into supporting woman suffrage. Many of the picketers were arrested and jailed.

With 2 million members, NAWSA itself was now the largest women's voluntary organization in the country. As their cause made increasingly visible progress and their work intensified, suffragists grew more and more exhilarated.

In 1917, the war intervened in the rush to the finish line. Carrie Chapman Catt and the NAWSA leadership decided that the most appropriate response to the national crisis would be to throw NAWSA's support behind the war effort and, at the same time, to continue the fight for suffrage. Those who disagreed could quietly step aside. Catt herself resigned from the Woman's Peace Party that she had helped to found and encouraged NAWSA members to aid in war work. NAWSA funded and sponsored a hospital in France, and both Catt and Anna Howard Shaw served on the Women's Council for the National Defense, which was organized to integrate women into conservation, farming, and other kinds of war relief work.

A cooperative stance on the war effort gained NAWSA many valuable supporters, and it put President Wilson in their debt. A stunning victory in New York State late in 1917 not only confirmed the positive popular response to NAWSA's war work, it also brought suffragists the electoral power of the largest state in the Northeast.

Leaders of the more militant National Woman's Party decided against official participation in the war effort. They stepped up their

A pamphlet containing Carrie Chapman Catt's speech for NAWSA's 1917 national convention in Washington, D.C. Catt did not deliver this address to Congress, but each senator and representative received a copy, which argued that woman suffrage was a matter of logic and justice.

picketing and carried increasingly provocative placards, which called the President "Kaiser Wilson" and accused him of betraying democracy by continuing to exclude women. Skirmishes with male on-lookers led to the arrests of more than 200 picketers in the summer and fall of 1917. Nearly half of these women went to jail. There they were treated roughly amid miserable living conditions. Like their British sisters, the women demanded to be classed as political prisoners, and when political status was denied, a number of them went on a hunger strike. Force-feedings made front page news. Within weeks, a huge public outcry about the treatment of these American suffragists embarrassed the authorities into releasing them.

Leaders in NAWSA and their allies in Congress quickly distanced themselves from the militant suffragists of the National Woman's Party. Catt denied any connection with the other group, although they were fighting for the same cause, and she did not protest their brutal treatment. In the end, however, the episode helped rather than hurt the suffrage cause. First, it was a tremendous source of publicity, and second, many Americans were appalled that such outrages had been perpetrated against women peacefully demanding their rights in a democratic country. Many others—including some cautious congressmen who had been sitting on the fence—simply decided to embrace the more conservative suffragists of NAWSA as the lesser of two evils.

Mary Church Terrell and her daughter were among the few African-American women who joined the picketers around the White House, though they were not arrested. Black women, in general, continued to pursue suffrage in segregated organizations and through a growing number of black woman suffrage leagues in the North and the South. Such leagues were repeatedly snubbed by the leaders of both NAWSA and the National Woman's Party, who were still trying to win support for suffrage in the South and among Southern senators and congressmen.

In early 1918, the suffragists and members of both political parties realized that the woman suffrage amendment finally had enough support to make it through the House of Representatives. President Wilson advised fellow Democrats to vote for the amendment "as an act of right and justice to the women of the country and of the world." On the morning of January 10, Jeannette Rankin rose in the main

Women lobbied members of Congress on the steps of the Capitol to vote for the suffrage amendment. At right, a cartoon shows a lobbyist working the Senate corridors just after the House passed the amendment in January 1918.

chamber of the House to introduce the Anthony Amendment, as it had been called for many years. Women from both NAWSA and the National Woman's Party packed the visitors' galleries, waiting anxiously; they knew that they had not a single vote to spare. One congressional supporter, who was very ill, was brought in on a stretcher to cast his vote; another man had broken his shoulder but waited to go to the hospital to have it set until after the vote was taken. A New York congressman came from the bedside of his dying wife, who was a suffragist and had insisted that he go. He returned to New York after the vote to attend her funeral. When at last the vote was tallied, it won by 274 to 136, exactly the two-thirds majority required to pass a constitutional amendment. Momentarily stunned by their first national victory, the women started to leave the gallery, and then spontaneously broke into a hymn of praise that filled the House chamber and echoed through the hallways.

The suffrage amendment moved on to the Senate, where it would remain bogged down for a year and a half before the women could muster sufficient votes to ensure the needed two-thirds majority. In the 1918 elections, NAWSA worked systematically to defeat four anti-suffrage senators, and the National Woman's Party once again took up its picketing campaign.

Black women's suffrage organizations continued to pursue some measure of just treatment or inclusion from white suffragists. In 1919, hoping to demonstrate the political power their organizations had amassed, the NACW's Northeastern Federation of Colored Women's Clubs applied for membership in NAWSA. The leaders of NAWSA panicked. How would the addition of 6,000 black women to their ranks look to the Southern senators whose votes they were courting? Pleading the need for political expediency, NAWSA's embarrassed leaders begged the federation to postpone its application. Ultimately, the federation agreed to withdraw in exchange for a promise from NAWSA that it would not support any last-minute attempts to rewrite the constitutional amendment to include a states' enforcement clause. (Such a clause, tacked on to the Anthony Amendment, would state that the separate states, rather than Congress, had the power to enforce the provisions of the new law. State control over enforcement would make it possible for Southern states to find ways to keep black women from voting.)

In June 1919, after a string of negative votes, the Senate finally approved the suffrage measure. Scarcely pausing for breath, suffragists fanned out across the country to help secure the needed ratification by three-quarters of the states. In less than a year, 35 of the necessary 36 states had ratified the amendment. National attention then focused on Tennessee, the only remaining state in which anti-suffrage was not so firmly entrenched as to make ratification impossible. Still, the opposition was fierce, and representatives of the anti-suffrage interests poured into the state capital of Nashville, alternately threatening the legislators and plying them with liquor.

Today, the image of women and men entering the polling place together attracts no notice. But when this early photo was taken following the passage of the 19th Amendment, it was a newsworthy event.

On the last day of the special session, the vote came down to a single undecided representative, 24-year-old Harry Burn, the youngest member of the legislature. Just hours before the vote, Burn had received a letter from his mother, a suffrage supporter, urging him to "be a good boy and help Mrs. Catt put 'Rat' in Ratification." Burn voted "Yes," and the amendment passed. A few days later, on August 26, 1920, the Secretary of State issued a formal proclamation declaring the elective franchise to be the right of every adult woman citizen of the United States. It had been 72 years, one month, and one week since the meeting in Seneca Falls, New York, on July 19, 1848, when American women had first convened to demand their "sacred right" to vote.

Exhausted and elated, suffragists shared a moment of accord, though there would be no permanent unity in the women's movement in the decades to come and, for many years, no women's victories as spectacularly satisfying as the achievement of suffrage. An English suffragist might have been speaking for her American sisters when she wrote: "All the time, watching, attacking, defending, moving, and counter-moving! . . . how glorious . . . those days were! To lose the personal in the great impersonal is to live!"

For the rest of their lives, suffragists and other Progressive women would remember the years of struggle and female solidarity with powerful nostalgia. Not only had the work itself been liberating, but women could point to real changes that they had made in American society and politics between 1890 and 1920. It was American women opening doors, pushing at the boundaries of traditional roles, emerging into public life in unprecedented numbers, that had set the tone and the agenda for those reforms in labor, politics, and urban life that became the dominant characteristic of the Progressive Era. Looking at the long years that lay ahead in the 20th century, at the new campaigns for justice and equality that would demand their attention, American women could confidently tell one another they had made a splendid beginning.

CHRONOLOGY

1890	Wyoming enters the Union, becoming the only state with full woman suffrage; Creation of the National American Woman Suffrage Association (NAWSA) and of the General Federation of Women's Clubs (GFWC)
1892	Ellis Island opens for immigration screening
1893	World's Columbian Exposition in Chicago
1894	Coxey's Army of the unemployed marches on Washington, D.C.; Pullman strike temporarily cripples railroads
1896	Supreme Court decision *Plessy* v. *Ferguson* institutionalizes segregation of black and white Americans in "separate but equal" public facilities; Creation of the National Association of Colored Women (NACW)
April-December 1898	The Spanish-American War
September 1901	President William McKinley is assassinated; Theodore Roosevelt becomes President
1903	Wright brothers fly first airplane at Kitty Hawk, N.C.; Founding of Women's Trade Union League (WTUL)
April 18, 1906	San Francisco earthquake
1909	Henry Ford markets the Model T, the first car made on an assembly line; Founding of the National Association for the Advancement of Colored People (NAACP)
March 25, 1911	Triangle Shirtwaist Factory fire in New York City
1912	Sinking of the luxury liner *Titanic* on its first voyage from England to America
1914	World War I begins in Europe; Founding of Congressional Union, later known as National Woman's Party
1915	First long-distance telephone call, from New York to California
1917	United States declares war on Germany and enters World War II
1918-1920	Red Scare sweeps the United States, resulting in many arrests and deportations
November 11, 1918	Armistice signed that ends World War II
1919	League of Nations established; 18th Amendment outlaws sale and consumption of alcohol
August 26, 1920	19th Amendment, granting woman suffrage, is ratified

FURTHER READING

A Note on Sources

In the interest of readability, the volumes in this series include no discussion of historiography and no footnotes. As works of synthesis and overview, however, they are greatly indebted to the research and writing of other historians. The principal works drawn on in this volume are among the books listed below.

General Histories of Women

Cirksena, J. Diane, and Valija Rasmussen. *Women in Progressive America 1890–1920: Social Reconstruction.* St. Louis Park, Minn.: Upper Midwest Women's History Center, 1991.

Clinton, Catherine. *The Other Civil War: American Women in the Nineteenth Century.* New York: Hill & Wang, 1984.

Cott, Nancy F. *The Bonds of Womanhood: "Woman's Sphere" in New England, 1780–1835.* New Haven: Yale University Press, 1977.

DuBois, Ellen Carol, and Vicki L. Ruiz. *Unequal Sisters: A Multicultural Reader in U.S. Women's History.* New York: Routledge, Chapman & Hall, 1990.

Evans, Sara. *Born for Liberty: A History of Women in America.* New York: Free Press, Macmillan, 1989.

Friedman, Jean E., and William G. Shade, eds. *Our American Sisters: Women in American Life and Thought.* Boston: Allyn & Bacon, 1973 and 1976.

Greenwald, Maurine Weiner. *Women, War, and Work: The Impact of World War I on Women Workers in the United States.* Westport, Conn.: Greenwood Press, 1980.

James, Edward, Janet Wilson James, and Paul Boyer, eds. *Notable American Women, 1607–1950: A Biographical Dictionary.* Cambridge: Belknap Press of Harvard University Press, 1971.

Kerber, Linda K., and Jane Sherron DeHart. *Women's America: Refocusing the Past.* 3rd ed. New York: Oxford University Press, 1991.

Lerner, Gerda, ed. *Black Women in White America: A Documentary History.* New York: Random House, 1973. New edition, 1993.

———, ed. *The Female Experience: An American Documentary.* New York: Oxford University Press, 1992.

Niethammer, Carolyn. *Daughters of the Earth: The Lives and Legends of American Indian Women.* New York: Collier Macmillan, 1977.

Norton, Mary Beth, ed. *Major Problems in American Women's History: Documents and Essays.* Lexington, Mass.: D.C. Heath, 1989.

Rappaport, Doreen. *American Women, Their Lives in Their Words.* New York: Harper Collins Children's Books, 1990.

Riley, Glenda. *Inventing the American Woman, A Perspective on Women's History 1865 to the Present.* Arlington Heights, Ill.: Harlan Davidson, 1986.

Scott, Anne Firor. *The Southern Lady: From Pedestal to Politics 1830–1930.* Chicago: University of Chicago Press, 1970.

World's Columbian Exposition

Holley, Marietta (Josiah Allen's wife). *Samantha at the World's Fair.* New York: Funk & Wagnalls, 1893.

Schlereth, Thomas J. *Victorian America: Transformations in Everyday Life 1876–1915.* New York: Harper Collins, 1991.

Weimann, Jeanne Madeline. *The Fair Women.* Chicago: Academy Chicago, 1981.

Domestic Life

Abbott, Shirley. *Womenfolks: Growing Up Down South.* New York: Ticknor & Fields, 1983.

Cather, Willa Silbert. *O Pioneers!* Boston: Houghton Mifflin, 1913.

Cowan, Ruth Schwartz. *More Work for Mother: The Ironies of Household Technology from the Open Hearth to the Microwave.* New York: Basic Books, 1983.

Davis, Angela Y. *Women, Race, and Class.* New York: Random House, 1981.

Degler, Carl. *At Odds: Women and the Family in America from the Revolution to the Present.* New York: Oxford University Press, 1980.

Dudden, Faye E. *Serving Women: Household Service in Nineteenth-Century America.* Middletown, Conn.: Wesleyan University Press, 1983.

Ewen, Elizabeth. *Immigrant Women in the Land of Dollars: Life and Culture on the Lower East Side 1890–1925.* New York: Monthly Review Press, 1985.

Hayden, Dolores. *The Grand Domestic Revolution: A History of Feminist Designs for American Homes, Neighborhoods, and Cities.* Cambridge: MIT Press, 1981.

Jones, Jacqueline. *Labor of Love, Labor of Sorrow: Black Women, Work, and the Family from Slavery to the Present.* New York: Basic Books, 1985.

Matthews, Glenna. *Just a Housewife: The Rise and Fall of Domesticity in America.* New York: Oxford University Press, 1987.

Ogden, Annegret S. *The Great American Housewife: From Helpmate to Wage Earner, 1776–1986.* Westport, Conn.: Greenwood Press, 1986.

Peiss, Kathy. *Cheap Amusements: Working Women and Leisure in Turn-of-the-Century New York.* Philadelphia: Temple University Press, 1986.

Shapiro, Laura. *Perfection Salad: Women and Cooking at the Turn of the Century.* New York: Farrar, Strauss & Giroux, 1986.

Sklar, Kathryn Kish. *Catharine Beecher: A Study in American Domesticity.* New York: Norton, 1976.

Strasser, Susan. *Never Done: A History of American Housework.* New York: Pantheon, 1982.

Terrell, Mary Church. *A Colored Woman in a White World.* Washington, D.C.: Ransdell, 1940.

Weatherford, Doris. *Foreign and Female: Immigrant Women in America 1840–1930.* New York: Schocken Books, 1986.

Yezierska, Anzia. *Breadgivers.* 1925. Reprint. New York: Persea Books, 1975.

Women and Work

Baxandall, Rosalyn, Linda Gordon, and Susan Reverby, eds. *America's Working Women: A Documentary History—1600 to the Present.* New York: Random House, 1976.

Brody, David. *Workers in Industrial America: Essays on the 20th Century Struggle.* New York: Oxford University Press, 1980.

Katzman, David M. *Seven Days a Week: Women and Domestic Service in Industrializing America.* New York: Oxford University Press, 1978.

Kessler-Harris, Alice. *Out to Work: A History of Wage-Earning Women in the United States.* New York: Oxford University Press, 1982.

Richardson, Dorothy. *The Long Day, The Story of a New York City Working Girl.* 1905. Reprint. Edited by Cindy Sondik Aron. Charlottesville: University of Virginia Press, 1990.

Tax, Meredith. *The Rising of the Women: Feminist Solidarity and Class Conflict, 1880–1917.* New York: Monthly Review Press, 1980.

Wertheimer, Barbara Mayer. *We Were There: The Story of Working Women in America.* New York: Pantheon Books, 1977.

Women in Public Life

Davis, Allen F. *American Heroine: The Life and Legend of Jane Addams.* New York: Oxford University Press, 1973.

————. *Spearheads for Reform: The Social Settlements and the Progressive Movement, 1890–1914.* New York: Oxford University Press, 1967.

Dobkin, Marjorie Housepian. *The Making of a Feminist: Early Journals and Letters of M. Carey Thomas.* Kent, Ohio: Kent State University Press, 1979.

Flexner, Eleanor. *Century of Struggle: The Woman's Rights Movement in the United States.* New York: Atheneum, 1972.

Frankfort, Roberta. *Collegiate Women: Domesticity and Career in Turn-of-the-Century America.* New York: New York University Press, 1977.

Giddings, Paula. *When and Where I Enter: The Impact of Black Women on Race and Sex in America.* New York: William Morrow, 1984.

Kraditor, Aileen S. *The Ideas of the Woman Suffrage Movement, 1890–1920.* New York: Columbia University Press, 1965.

Peavy, Linda, and Ursula Smith. *Women Who Changed Things.* New York: Scribners, 1983.

Solomon, Barbara Miller. *In the Company of Educated Women: A History of Women and Higher Education in America.* New Haven: Yale University Press, 1985.

Van Voris, Jacqueline. *Carrie Chapman Catt: A Public Life.* New York: Feminist Press at the City University of New York, 1987.

Ware, Susan. *Partner and I: Molly Dewson, Feminism, and New Deal Politics.* New Haven: Yale University Press, 1987.

Rebels

Blair, Fredrika. *Isadora: Portrait of the Artist as a Woman.* New York: McGraw Hill, 1986.

Cott, Nancy. *The Grounding of Modern Feminism.* New Haven: Yale University Press, 1987.

Drinnon, Richard. *Rebel in Paradise: A Biography of Emma Goldman.* Boston: Beacon Press, 1961.

Duncan, Isadora. *My Life*. Garden City, N.Y.: Garden City Publishing, 1927.

Gilman, Charlotte Perkins. *Herland*. Edited by Ann J. Lane. New York: Pantheon Books, 1979. First published in "The Forerunner," 1915.

———. *Women and Economics: The Economic Factor Between Men and Women as a Factor in Social Evolution*. Edited by Carl Degler. New York: Harper & Row, 1966. Originally published in Boston: Small, Maynard, 1898.

Gordon, Linda. *Woman's Body, Woman's Right: A Social History of Birth Control in America*. New York: Grossman, 1976.

Lane, Ann J. *To Herland and Beyond: The Life and Work of Charlotte Perkins Gilman*. New York: Pantheon, 1990.

May, Henry F. *The End of American Innocence: A Study of the First Years of Our Own Time 1912–1917*. New York: Knopf, 1959.

Sanger, Margaret. *My Fight for Birth Control*. Elmsford, N.Y.: Maxwell Reprint edition, 1969.

Topalian, Elyse. *Margaret Sanger*. New York: Franklin Watts, 1984.

Wexler, Alice. *Emma Goldman, An Intimate Life*. New York: Pantheon, 1984.

INDEX

Acknowledgments

In addition to the books and authors previously listed, I would like to acknowledge the following, whose ideas and articles have significantly influenced the shape and content of this book: Ruth Bordin, Joan Jacobs Brumberg, Blanche Wiesen Cook, Helen Lefkowitz Horowitz, William O'Neill, Anne F. Scott and Andrew M. Scott, Kathryn Kish Sklar, Carol Smith Rosenberg, Daniel Scott Smith, Barbara Welter, and Jean Willis. I would also like to thank my friend and colleague, Joyce Berkman, who patiently supplied many references and helped me to deal with some difficult questions. My special thanks to series editor Nancy Cott, who has guided my part of this project with consummate tact and great scholarly generosity.

Picture Credits

Karen Manners Smith holds degrees from Brandeis University and the University of Massachusetts. Her fields are American women's history and biography. She is currently completing a life of Mary Virginia Terhune: *"Marion Harland": The Making of a Household Word,* and has delivered papers on Terhune at Winterthur Museum, Radcliffe College, and the 1994 Conference on Southern Women's History at Rice University. Dr. Smith has taught U.S. women's history at Smith College.

Nancy F. Cott is Stanley Woodward Professor of history and American studies at Yale University. She is the author of *The Bonds of Womanhood: "Woman's Sphere" in New England 1780–1835, The Grounding of Modern Feminism,* and *A Woman Making History: Mary Ritter Beard Through Her Letters;* editor of *Root of Bitterness: Documents of the Social History of American Women;* and co-editor of *A Heritage of Her Own: Toward a New Social History of American Women.*